Edie MacKenzie

Goldendoodles

Everything About Purchase,
Care, Nutrition, Behavior,
and Training

BARRON'S

CONTENTS

AN INTRODUCTION TO GOLDENDOODLES

The Goldendoodle is a purposefully bred hybrid that, unfortunately, is lumped into the category of "Designer Dog." In my opinion, they are not Designer Dogs, but rather, dogs of good design.

Goldendoodles are the result of the purposeful breeding of Golden Retrievers and Poodles and were first bred in the 1990s. Being a hybrid of two of the most intelligent dog breeds, Goldendoodles are very smart. You could even say they are somewhat "high maintenance" if not intellectually stimulated and properly trained. If you decide to bring a Goldendoodle into your life, be prepared to spend time with them, because these dogs do not flourish if left by themselves for most of the day. These are highly social dogs who are very people oriented and need a good amount of human interaction.

Goldendoodles have an intuitive, sensitive nature—a genetic gift from their Golden Retriever parent. In addition to their superior intelligence, the Poodle parent often contributes a nonshedding, allergy-friendly coat.

Goldendoodles are athletic dogs and require moderate exercise. Their athleticism has led them to excel in various competitive canine sports, most notably Agility. It would not be a surprise to hear one day that Goldendoodles excel as gundogs or field dogs. Goldendoodles are soft-mouthed retrievers that love water sports!

Goldendoodles are gaining in popularity, because of their intelligence, playfulness, and, depending on the Goldendoodle, sometimes allergy-friendly coats. They have oodles of energy and boast an entertaining personality.

But why breed them? Well, throughout history man has bred dogs to meet a need within the human community. All you have to do is stroll down any street to see all of the different breeds created to fill a human need. For example, the giant Newfoundland was bred to

pull nets for fishermen in the frigid North Atlantic. The Dachshund was bred to dig for and hunt badgers. Poodles, originally bred as water dogs, were used to retrieve waterfowl. And even the original lapdog, the Tibetan Spaniel, was bred to warm the bodies of Buddhist monks while they prayed.

The Goldendoodle, along with its cousin the Labradoodle, was developed to serve as an allergy-friendly service and therapy dog. They have successfully allowed people in need of a service dog, but who suffer with dog allergies, to finally get the help they need to make life more manageable.

And like the Golden Retriever, and many other dogs who no longer perform the services they were bred for, most Goldendoodles live the life of a beloved pet. However, that does not negate the importance and the life-changing benefits these dogs bring to those needing their allergy-friendly coat and their willingness to serve. A small but significant number do perform the work for which they were developed; their inherently intuitive nature and keen intellect allows them to excel in the areas of service and therapy work. And because they often have nonshedding, allergy-friendly coats, they are able to reach a wider group of people who are finally able to get the service dog they need.

Goldendoodles are very adaptable and fit well into almost any family environment. Although their high intelligence can lead to boredom and therefore mischief, well-bred Goldendoodles have an easygoing personality that makes them wonderful for young families or people without a great deal of experience raising dogs.

Once again their intelligence and intuitive nature come into play when you are training

TIP

More than one owner has found their Goldendoodle to be a bit too smart. Don't be fooled into thinking a smart dog requires less training and work. Quite the opposite. A highly intelligent dog like the Goldendoodle requires more intellectual stimulation and socialization than other dogs.

your Goldendoodle. They are quick learners and shine in any kind of training environment. You often hear Goldendoodle owners talk about their puppy or dog being the "model" student in the class and often used by the instructor to demonstrate how something should be done.

When training your Goldendoodle, you need to "mix it up." Your Goldendoodle will discern patterns. If your training pattern consists of *sit, down,* and *roll over,* you'll quickly find your Goldendoodle demonstrating the entire sequence when you tell her to *sit.* Once you have finished laughing, try to think of ways you can change the routine.

As I just mentioned, Goldendoodles love to please. They have a way of tilting their head and looking at you, as if trying to figure out what you want next. With the Poodle intelligence and Golden Retriever intuitiveness, your Goldendoodle can read you like a book. It is up to you to learn to send her the right messages.

So, let's begin by exploring whether a Goldendoodle is the right dog for you and your family. . . .

ABOUT THE GOLDENDOODLE

So what exactly is a Goldendoodle? A basic understanding of the Goldendoodle will help you decide if it is the right dog for you. And if it is, learn about the importance of knowing how to choose the right breeder and puppy.

The Goldendoodle is a hybrid dog created by mating a Golden Retriever with a Poodle. When two unrelated breeds of the same species reproduce, their offspring experience what is known as hybrid vigor, whereby they receive all of the parents' good traits and few of the bad. This works as long as the parent breeds do not have a common gene for a genetic defect. (Hybrid vigor and a number of parental health issues, along with parental health testing, are all discussed in detail in Chapter 4.)

A Little History

The Golden Retriever

The Golden Retriever was developed in Scotland in the mid-nineteenth century as a retriever for both upland game and waterfowl. They were bred to have a soft mouth and a dense, water-repellant coat. Although prized for their stamina in the field, it is their intelligence, trainability, and amiable, eager-to-please nature that has made them one of the most popular companion dogs in the world.

There are two types of Golden Retrievers. The English Golden Retriever has a stocky, heavier build with a blocky head, whereas the American Golden Retriever is a taller, finer-boned dog with a narrower head.

The Poodle

Although Poodles are the national dog of France, it is believed that they originated in Germany or Russia. The Poodle, as we know it today, first appears in fifteenth-and sixteenth-century art work. With their curly, allergy-friendly, dense coat, confident air, and biddable nature, Poodles were originally bred to retrieve waterfowl. During the nineteenth century the

Poodle became the dog of aristocracy, eventually being bred to the three recognized size variations—standard, miniature, and toy—we recognize today. Highly intelligent, easy to

train, and eager to please, Poodles are excellent companion dogs.

The Goldendoodle

Goldendoodles have been purposefully bred since the mid-1990s. When well bred, they are wonderful, calm, often allergy-friendly, family pets. Many Goldendoodles also work as allergy-friendly service and therapy dogs because their gentle, intuitive nature makes them well suited for this work.

The Goldendoodle Personality

The Goldendoodle's personality is a reflection of the Golden Retriever's, generally a warm and fuzzy type. And, along with the Golden Retriever's intuitive nature, Goldendoodles are attentive dogs. Their Poodle parent brings to the Goldendoodle a very high level of canine intelligence.

Hybrid vigor, the pairing of different breeds within a species, does, in theory, produces healthier puppies; however, it is not a guarantee. (Hybrid vigor is discussed further in Chapter 4.) Let me stress, you need to be *very careful* when choosing your breeder and puppy.

Goldendoodles can be a good choice for people with limited experience raising a dog because they are happy and affectionate with a zestful "life of the party" personality. They'll come into your space immediately and are happy to visit with you. They have an eagerness to please and will make a great deal of eye contact trying to figure out what you want them to do. Couple this with their high level of intelligence and you have a dog that is relatively easy to train. However, their intelligence and enthusiastic nature requires diligence on your part. Contrary to popular belief, an intelligent dog requires more training and more stimulation than an average dog.

Because of their strong retriever parentage, Goldendoodles are mouthy, which means their mouth is more active when they are puppies, and they will use that mouth on you, or your children, if not properly trained. An easy way to train your Goldendoodle is to use her natural tendency to retrieve items. Whenever she gets mouthy with you or a family member, put a toy in her mouth; in no time, she will be greeting you at the door with a toy in her mouth.

Your Goldendoodle's temperament is determined by the parent dogs; however, regardless of her parents' fine temperaments, it is important to understand that all puppies, no matter the breed, are busy and active, and Goldendoodles are no exception. Often their mellow,

calm temperament becomes more apparent as they approach maturity, which is why it is essential to work with a breeder who is actively breeding for health and calm temperaments.

It is very important that prospective owners take their time to research carefully before purchasing a puppy so they get the one that meets their needs. If you find a reputable, respectable Goldendoodle breeder, you will find a puppy that will be a joy to have in your home.

Goldendoodle Coat Types

As a rule of thumb, the curlier the coat, the less likely it is to shed and induce an allergic reaction. This is why the Poodle is considered an allergy-friendly dog. The Goldendoodle's hair grows to 4 to 6 inches (10–15cm) long and

═══════ TIP ═══════

Adaptability

Goldendoodles are very adaptable to a family environment and, when properly trained, make good companion dogs for children.

usually has a wavy or curly look to it. More curl equals less shedding, so the straighter the coat, the higher the shedding. Based on her previous experience, your breeder should be able to give you a good idea about your puppy's adult coat.

The Types of Goldendoodles

Goldendoodles are a cross between a Golden Retriever and a Poodle. This type of breeding results in a litter of "F1" (*F* stands for the Latin word *filial* or *generation*) puppies or First Generation. F1 Goldendoodles generally have more consistently allergy-friendly coats than their cousins, the F1 Labradoodle, and because of this tendency, Goldendoodle breeders rarely breed beyond the initial pairing of the Golden Retriever and the Poodle. However, it is important to know about the different types of Goldendoodles and the potential health issues associated with each type.

Ideally, the breeders of Goldendoodles should breed for sound, genetically healthy dogs with a good, gentle temperament; however, you need to practice your due diligence, as the sudden popularity of the Goldendoodle has motivated many unscrupulous breeders. Popularity

is one of the worst things that can happen to a dog breed. Please carefully read the section later in this chapter on how to choose a breeder. It will make a significant difference in the quality of the dog you take home.

The F1, F1B, F2, and Mini Goldendoodles

F1: The F1 Goldendoodle is the breeding of a Golden Retriever and a Poodle.

F1 Advantages: The main advantage of an F1 breeding is that the puppies have the highest possibilities of hybrid vigor and a reduced risk of genetic defects if both parents are health tested and are clear of any risk factors.

A well-bred F1 Goldendoodle has a delightful temperament and is a quick learner.

F1 Disadvantages: The primary disadvantage of F1 breeding is a higher risk of shedding because of a straighter coat, which is potentially problematic for someone with allergies.

F1B: The F1B Goldendoodle is the breeding of an F1 Goldendoodle, back-crossed (B) with a Poodle. This yields a dog 25 percent Golden Retriever and 75 percent Poodle.

F1B Advantages: The main advantage of F1B breeding is that these dogs have a higher probability of minimal shedding. By adding more Poodle into the genetic mix, the likelihood of a curly, non-allergy-inducing coat is much higher.

F1B Disadvantages: The most important disadvantage of F1B breeding is that these dogs may have reduced hybrid vigor and higher risks of genetic defects if the breeder doesn't conduct a careful background history of the parents. The Poodle used to back-cross to the F1 Goldendoodle must have no relationship whatsoever with the Poodle used to breed the F1 Goldendoodle; otherwise the probability of

recessive genetic flaws linking up is significantly increased.

F2: The F2 Goldendoodle results when both parents are F1 Goldendoodles. Although this yields a dog that is 50 percent Golden Retriever and 50 percent Poodle, the F2 is a more genetically diverse dog than the F1.

F2 Advantages: The primary advantage of F2 breeding is the ability to select the most desirable traits from a breeder's F1 Goldendoodles and reproduce them consistently.

F2 Disadvantages: The chief disadvantage of F2 breeding is the same as F1B; however, it is exacerbated by the need for the breeder to do a complete and thorough background check on the lineage of not only the Poodle lines used, but the Golden Retriever lines as well. This involves a high level of commitment on the part of a breeder, and quite frankly, few are willing to do it. It is imperative that no familial relationship exist within the lineage of either F2 Goldendoodle parent.

English "Teddy Bear" Goldendoodle

This is a Goldendoodle whose Golden Retriever parent is an English Golden Retriever. The blockier head from the English Golden Retriever gives the puppies a teddy bear quality, hence the nickname. When looking at an English Goldendoodle, make sure the breeder has documented proof of the European ancestry of the English Golden Retriever. There are breeders who will sell Teddy Bear Goldendoodles that do not originate from true English Golden Retrievers.

Goldendoodle Sizes

Standard and Miniature

There are two typical sizes for the Goldendoodle: standard and miniature. The breeding of a Golden Retriever and a Standard Poodle results in the Standard Goldendoodle, which is a medium to large-sized dog. Males are typically 21–29 inches (50–73 cm) tall with a weight of 55–90 pounds. Females are typically 20–25 inches (50–63 cm) tall with a weight of 45–65 pounds. However, it is not uncommon for a Goldendoodle to weigh more than 100 pounds (45 kg).

Miniature Goldendoodles are small to medium-sized dogs, depending on the Poodle used to sire; therefore, the size range is quite wide. A Toy Poodle sire results in a smaller dog than a Miniature Poodle sire. The height range for a Miniature Goldendoodle is 13–21 inches (32.5–52.5 cm), and the weight range is 25–45 pounds (11–20 kg).

Goldendoodle Colors

Contrary to their name, Goldendoodles can come in a variety of colors. The most common colors are cream and gold, but many Goldendoodles are also chocolate or black. Less common, but rather striking, are the red Goldendoodles. Parti Goldendoodles are generally

— TIP —

An experienced breeder can tell you approximately how big your Goldendoodle puppy will be when she reaches maturity.

white with large blocks of either black or brown. The parti coloring comes from the Poodle parent. Also, a Goldendoodle will, on occasion, have either black phantom or chocolate phantom coloring. This is because of the phantom coloring in the genetics of the Poodle parent. There is also the rare and beautiful silver color, the coloring for which, again, comes from the Poodle parent.

Choosing a Breeder

It is important to purchase your puppy from a trustworthy and experienced breeder, and that comes with a heftier cost. However, if you are looking for a top-quality Goldendoodle, price should be at the bottom of your priority list. You know you have found a good breeder if the person's mission is to produce healthy, sound, well-tempered dogs. Finding a good breeder can be a long and tedious process, but it's worth every minute of research if you find the right breeder who can provide you with the right Goldendoodle.

Finding the right breeder is especially critical with Goldendoodles. There are countless backyard breeders doing it solely for the money, with no real attention to the critical issues of health and temperament.

The reputable breeder strives to advance the quality of the puppies with each new litter. This breeder matches parent dogs based on certain criteria, which include desirable physical and behavioral characteristics, to produce a healthy litter. Warning! All puppies are cute! Visit as many breeders as possible before selecting a puppy and don't be tempted to buy a puppy on your first visit; it is too easy to get caught up in the excitement of seeing all the precious pups.

=== TIP ===

A Word About Puppy Mills

Unfortunately, puppy mills (large, commercial dog-breeding facilities) are a big business. Dogs are poorly treated, live in filthy, confined conditions, and receive little or no veterinary care. They don't get any exercise, playtime, or companionship. They often endure mistreatment and malnutrition. Then, these dogs reproduce with each other, resulting in severe genetic defects and health problems. The puppies are seldom healthy.

Puppy mills typically sell their dogs in one of three ways: websites, pet stores, or through brokers who in turn sell the puppies to pet stores. Although not all puppies sold in pet stores come from puppy mills, a disturbing number of them do, so before you purchase a Goldendoodle puppy from a pet store, ask for the name and address of the breeder or the breeding facility (not the broker who may be the go-between), then go home and do some research. A quick Internet search will let you know if there are any complaints against them.

For more information about puppy mills and how to avoid purchasing a puppy-mill puppy (and thereby supporting this awful business), go to the Humane Society of the United States' site *www.stoppuppymills.org* or the America Society for the Prevention of Cruelty to Animals' (ASPCA) site *www.aspca.org* under "Fight Animal Cruelty." Both sites give excellent information about puppy mills, how they operate, and their sophisticated efforts to defraud consumers.

Visiting the breeders gives you an opportunity to meet the puppy's siblings and the parents so you get an idea of their physical and behavioral characteristics. Pay close attention to the parents to see if they are healthy and well behaved. Also, ask about their temperament and if they've had any type of health issues. (Parental health testing is discussed in depth in Chapter 4.) Take notice of how the puppies interact with the breeder. It is a good sign if they are playful and outgoing. If they are shy or fearful, there is a reason why.

Should a Breeder Be a Member of a Regulatory Body?

If a breeder is a member of a regulatory organization, you know that she/he has agreed to a code of ethics. However, few organizations can actually follow through to investigate whether the breeder is adhering to the code of ethics. Often they are limited to feedback and complaints.

If the breeder belongs to an association, it is helpful; however, lack of membership is not necessarily a bad thing. There are many ethical and responsible breeders who are not members of any regulatory body.

What's most important is the relationship you have with your breeder and the confidence you have in the person. When calling breeders, having a comfortable feeling with the person you're talking to can be a good indicator. It may not be the actual questions that matter most, but how the conversation goes and if you feel comfortable with the other person.

Questions to Ask the Breeder

When visiting Goldendoodle breeders, be well prepared with a list of questions. Here is a list the breeder should be happy to answer for you. If she/he is not cooperative in answering the questions, or acts annoyed, this might not be the breeder for you. A good breeder wants you to ask questions.

1. Ask why she is selling the puppies. Her response should give you a good idea if she is breeding for the love of Goldendoodles, or if she is trying to get rich off a high demand dog.

2. Ask many specific questions about the Goldendoodle breed, even if you already know the answers. This exercise will indicate how knowledgeable the breeder really is about the breed.

3. Ask what health testing has been done for the puppy. Has the puppy received her first vaccination? Has she been desexed?

4. Ask what health testing has been done for the puppy's parents.

5. Ask for a written copy of the puppy's health guarantee, and make sure the warranty is clear.

6. Ask the breeder how the puppies are socialized. Specifically, are they exposed to people, both adults and children, and other animals? How often is the puppy in social situations?

7. Ask the breeder what the puppy's diet has consisted of so far.

8. Ask if the breeder is listed with The Goldendoodle website, The Goldendoodle & Labradoodle Premium Breeders List, or the Goldendoodle Association of North America.

9. Ask if the puppy's parents are AKC registered.

10. Ask the breeder for references. If she does not encourage or allow you to talk to previous customers, be concerned. Be sure to get several references and call them.

11. Ask the breeder if you can contact her during the life of your Goldendoodle about any health or behavioral concerns.

Health Guarantees and Testing

The health guarantee is something a potential Goldendoodle purchaser can use to evaluate a breeder.

Make certain you are able to view and are given a written copy of the breeder's guarantee and contract before you send any deposit money. Many breeders and websites claim they guarantee their puppies but fail to follow through with any guarantee or provide you with a written copy, which can lead to problems of not knowing what is or isn't covered. Reputable breeders who are confident in their

puppies will be more than happy to provide you with this information before you send them any deposit money. Read the health guarantee and contract *very* carefully and make sure you are comfortable with all of the terms. For example, if a legitimate genetic defect is found, will you be required to return your puppy to the breeder? Or will the breeder refund a portion of your purchase price to help defray some of the veterinary costs? Or will the person help to rehome your puppy, with a full release of its medical records, to another family better able to manage the health issues? What are you, the owner, required to do while raising your puppy to stay in compliance with the terms of the health guarantee? For example, some breeders require the puppy be fed a specific diet for the guarantee to remain valid.

I cannot stress enough the importance of reading and understanding the breeder's health guarantee. I recently heard of a breeder whose health guarantee was for *fatal* genetic flaws only. Given that, it can be assumed since something like hip dysplasia is not a *fatal* genetic flaw, it would not be covered in the guarantee. In my opinion, this is not acceptable. As the owner of the puppy, ensure your interests are covered, not just the interests of the breeder.

There are also unscrupulous breeders who charge extra for a health guarantee or regular veterinary checks. Again, this is not something reputable breeders do, and you, the consumer, need to exercise caution.

Goldendoodle Breeder Concerns

When considering a breeder, you need to confirm that the sire and dam are AKC registered and have successful PennHIP or OFA scores (see page 44). You will also want to be sure the sire and dam are well-tempered dogs. Be cautious! There are too many backyard breeders cashing in on the current popularity of Goldendoodles. I would highly recommend

---

If you see evidence of neglect and/or abuse of either the puppies or the parents, do not hesitate to contact the American Society for the Prevention of Cruelty to Animals at *www.aspca.org*.

Your voice may be the only one for the neglected animals.

---

posting an inquiry on one of the Doodle forums listed in the Information Section and asking for feedback on your list of potential breeders.

What to Expect from a Breeder

Just as you expect to buy a high-quality puppy from a top-notch breeder, the breeder should expect to sell only to a reliable caretaker who will bring the puppy into a loving home. You should feel like you are being interviewed by the breeder for the privilege of taking this puppy home. She should ask very specific questions in order to learn how you plan to care for the puppy. These questions are your indication that she is sincerely concerned about the puppy's well-being. If she seems more concerned about how you are going to pay for the pup, then it is likely the breeder is in the business for the wrong reasons.

If the puppy is less than six weeks old, the breeder should not allow you to hold her. This is for the puppy's health. The breeder should insist that the puppy not leave her mother before eight weeks. However, it is not uncommon for a good breeder to keep the puppies up to 12 weeks. It is important for the puppy to be close to her mother and littermates from ages four to eight weeks. She is learning how to interact, and if she's deprived of this essential developmental period, she could develop behavioral problems, such as aggression. Socialization with other people and animals should take place between 6 and 12 weeks of age.

After you purchase your Goldendoodle puppy, the breeder should encourage you to call her if there are any health or behavioral concerns. In fact, she should insist on it. This shows she cares about the puppies and is making an effort to improve the quality of future litters. The

---
TIP

Rescue Dogs

Are you interested in a rescue Golden-doodle? The International Doodle Owners Rescue/Rehome Resources may be able to help you. Check their website at *www.idog. biz/IDOGRRR.html.* You will find available dogs, an adoption application, and a variety of other information.

breeder should also require your contact information so she can contact you.

If the breeder does not allow you to see, at the minimum, the mother, this should be cause for concern. When you are visiting the breeders, take a look around the premises. The environment should be clean and safe. Ask to see where the puppies sleep and play. If the puppies are less than six weeks old and are not vaccinated, they should not be kept outdoors.

The puppies should be clean, well fed, healthy, energetic, and social. If they are dirty and foul smelling or have glassy eyes or runny noses, you should be apprehensive. And don't forget to check the cleanliness of the ears.

What to Expect on a Puppy Application

You should expect to fill out an application before purchasing your Goldendoodle. This form collects information about you and your family's desire for the puppy. Some potential questions are as follows:
- Why do you want a Goldendoodle?
- Have you ever owned or trained a dog before?

- Where will your puppy sleep?
- How many hours will she be left alone each day?
- What will you feed her?

There will also be questions about your family's dynamics, as well as questions about allergies within your family. At this point, you are usually required to pay a nonrefundable deposit. Typically, you pay the remainder of the fee when you take possession of the puppy. Again, make certain you have thoroughly read, and are comfortable with, the terms of the breeder's contract and health guarantee *before* you send any money.

NEW PUPPY, NOW WHAT?

You have decided to bring a Goldendoodle into your home. Are you ready? In this chapter we will discuss the preparations you will need to make before you bring your new bundle of fur home.

Bringing a Puppy into the Family

When is the best time to bring a Goldendoodle into your family? This is a very personal decision for each family and depends a great deal on your family life. You have to honestly ask yourself if there is enough time in your day to accommodate the puppy, and not just now, but 5, 10, and 15 years down the road. For some families, the decision to add a puppy is an easy yes. For others, sports, work schedules, school schedules, and any other number of activities outside the home may make the answer a no because the puppy would have to spend too much time alone and kenneled. Be honest with yourself about the amount of time you have to devote to a puppy, because a dog is a lifetime commitment!

If you feel you have time for a dog but not a puppy, consider an older rescue Goldendoodle. Also, breeders someitmes have dogs that, due to various issues within their original family, need to be rehomed.

Before Bringing Your Puppy Home

Plastic Kennel Versus Wire Kennel

Hard plastic kennels with "windows" for airflow come in a variety of sizes and provide an enclosed, more denlike environment. A wire kennel is a more open-style kennel that also comes in an assortment of sizes. Both kennels are safe, functional choices for your puppy's home. Whichever crate style you choose, it should have two latches, top and bottom, on the door. A single latch in the center can be dangerous, because a dog desperate to get out of a crate can force her head into the upper or lower area, get stuck, cut off the airflow, and die. If you plan to travel with your Goldendoodle, be aware that airlines require the hard plastic style and do not accept pets in wire kennels.

Sweet Dreams—Crate Comfort

Call me paranoid, but I am not a fan of putting bedding in a kennel with a puppy or a dog

with a history of chewing things up. Puppyhood is a time of intense chewing. It is far too easy for an unattended Goldendoodle to not only chew up the bedding, but also ingest it. This can have tragic consequences. (See Intestinal Blockages in Chapter 4.) Until you are confident your Goldendoodle will not chew her bedding, I would recommend nothing but a sturdy, chew-proof toy go in the kennel with her. If you do get a bed, make sure it is a chew-resistant version.

Puppy Toys—Make Them Sturdy!

Puppyhood is a time of intense chewing, so you want sturdy toys. You do not want your puppy swallowing chunks of rubber, plastic, bone, or stuffing! These can cause intestinal blockages, which can be life threatening.

Grooming Supplies

To begin, the only tools you need are a slicker brush, a double-sided comb, a nail trimmer, and a pair of safety-tip scissors. As your Goldendoodle grows and her adult coat comes in, you may need to add grooming tools that better fit her coat type. (Grooming is discussed in more detail in Chapter 3.)

Outdoor Considerations

It is never wise for your Goldendoodle to be off leash in an unfenced area, particularly if she is new to your home. Unfortunately, from your Goldendoodle's perspective, too many things out in the world are far more interesting than you. Hard on the ego, isn't it?

Your two choices in fencing are "invisible fencing" or traditional fencing.

Invisible fencing consists of an electrified underground cable encircling the area designated for your Goldendoodle. She will wear a special collar that emits a warning buzz and then a shock if she gets too close to the fence line. Now, there are a few problems associated

TIP

Controlling Your Puppy

No matter which type of fencing you choose, I highly recommend keeping your Goldendoodle puppy either leashed or tethered (never leave a tethered puppy unattended) until she is fairly reliable on the recall. "Catch the Puppy" is not a good game to play with your young puppy, as you need to stay in control as much as possible.

with invisible fencing. The main one is that if your Goldendoodle crosses the invisible fence line while in pursuit of something, she will not want to reenter the yard because of the shock she knows awaits her when she crosses the line. The other drawback to invisible fencing is while it may keep your dog in your yard, it does not keep other dogs or people out. The upside to an invisible fence is that there is nothing to block your view and it can be significantly cheaper than traditional fencing.

Traditional fencing provides the highest level of security for your Goldendoodle. It keeps her in the yard while leaving other dogs and people on the other side. Be sure the fence is too tall for your Goldendoodle to leap over, as these are athletic dogs and jumping over a fence is not out of the realm of possibility. If you have traditional fencing, it must go completely to the ground all along the fence line. You would be amazed how small a gap a puppy can wriggle through! Also, if you have children or absent-minded adults in your home, it is prudent to install an auto-close mechanism on the fence gates.

Create a Schedule

Have a family meeting and decide who is to be responsible for your Goldendoodle's food, water, walking, cleanup, grooming, and so on (knowing it is ultimately your responsibility). Keeping a regular schedule is good for the puppy and for those taking care of her. It helps you remember to take her out, and it prevents accidents.

Find a Veterinarian

Research your local veterinarians and find one *before* you bring your puppy home. Be sure to find a veterinarian offering service, care, and a philosophy you trust. Once you have found a veterinarian, make an appointment for the first day or two after you bring your Goldendoodle home for a thorough examination. (Finding a veterinarian is discussed further in Chapter 4.)

Expenses? Do Tell!

Growing and Growing and Growing . . .

As your puppy grows, you will need to purchase increasingly large gear for her. Collars and harnesses are of particular importance. Your puppy will grow *fast*!
• **Kennel:** Start with a smaller kennel with just enough room for your puppy to stand up and turn around. You can also purchase a larger kennel and block a portion of it off. You want your puppy to have only enough room to spread out comfortably; otherwise your pup will do her business in one end of the kennel and sleep in the other.
• **Collars/Harnesses:** Pay close attention to how your puppy's collar fits because puppies outgrow their collars and harnesses very

Archie at two months.

Archie at six months.

quickly. Expect to purchase three to four different sizes before your puppy reaches her final size.

• **Feeding Dishes:** You will want to keep your Goldendoodle's food dish somewhat narrow to avoid the ends of her ears becoming caked with food. To do this, you may need to purchase two or three different-size bowls as she grows.

• **Toys:** As your Goldendoodle grows, she is going to need age- and size-appropriate toys. What's more, she is going to destroy some toys along the way.

• **Dog Beds:** If you purchase a dog bed for your puppy, try to purchase a chew-resistant version. Chances are good your puppy will chew through a couple of beds before she reaches maturity, so be prepared to replace as necessary.

Veterinarian Bills—Be Prepared!

Veterinary bills are a part of pet ownership, so set aside money for regular and unexpected visits. Consider pet insurance as a way to offset some of your veterinary costs. Here are some of the expenses you can expect:

• Shots

• Flea and tick preventive

• Heartworm preventive

• Wellness visits

• Spaying and neutering (if not done by your breeder or shelter)

• The dreaded run to the after-hours-emergency veterinarian. I recommend calling before you dash to the clinic. I have avoided several expensive after-hours' visits by calling first and having the staff there give me instructions on what I could do at home until my veterinarian opened in the morning. Sometimes, what appears to be a critical situation to us isn't to a trained veterinary technician, veterinary nurse, or veterinarian.

Obedience Classes—A Must!

Enroll yourself and your puppy in an obedience class once your veterinarian clears her to attend. Obedience classes not only teach you how to train your dog, but are an invaluable socialization opportunity for your new Goldendoodle.

Puppy Play Groups

Puppy play groups are a great way to help socialize your puppy without her getting knocked down by much larger adult dogs. Many training centers offer these play groups to their clients. Also, check with your veterinary clinic to see if they offer a puppy socialization group. Again, your veterinarian must clear your Goldendoodle to attend any activity that involves other dogs or puppies.

Dog Walker

Because your Goldendoodle should not be confined for the entire day while you are at work, consider having a dog walker come and let your puppy out to do her business and to get some exercise along with a bit of play time.

Doggy Day Care

This is an excellent way to know your puppy is receiving attention and play and exercise during the day. Many doggy day cares now have webcams so you can check in on your baby. Your veterinarian must clear her to attend.

Archie at one year.

Books, Books, Books!

I highly recommend reading as much as you can about puppies, dogs, and dog training. The more you know, the more confident you will feel. Reading also provides you with alternative methods for raising your Goldendoodle since no method is 100 percent effective with 100 percent of dogs. Furthermore, what worked when your puppy was very young may not be as effective when she hits her rebellious teenage phase. Knowing that if method A doesn't work, you can try method B keeps you calmer and more successful in whatever methodology ultimately works for you and your Goldendoodle.

For the safety of your new Goldendoodle puppy and your possessions, it is very important to puppy-proof your home before you bring her home. A puppy needs to learn what is acceptable to chew, and until she has learned those lessons, everything is a chew toy.

Remember, your Goldendoodle puppy is going to grow! What passes for puppy-proof today will not be adequate in a month or two. Be aware of her ever-increasing size, range, and curiosity.

If you have never had a puppy or owned a dog, you may not realize how many things in your home can be hazardous to your Golden-doodle's health. The following list will help you make your home a safer place for your dog.

• Close doors or set up baby gates to rooms you don't want the puppy to get into.

• Get all plants and small pets (gerbils, guinea pigs, fish, lizards, and so on) out of puppy range.

• Get all electrical cords and curtain/shade pulls out of puppy range. Covers for electrical cords are advisable.

• Keep kids' toys picked up and out of puppy reach. Puppies do not know the difference between their toys and your daughter's brand new Barbie doll.

• Remote controls and pieces of video-game equipment (which often get left on the floor) need to be put in a secure location.

• Lift up your wastebaskets. Gross as it sounds, dogs love dirty tissues and other nasty things put in wastebaskets. It is like having their own disgusting, nose-level buffet.

• Keep a tight lid on your garbage. There are things in your garbage that can be deadly for your Goldendoodle. For example, if your dog gets into the garbage and eats the leftover chicken bones, they can do a tremendous amount of damage to her digestive tract.

• Goldendoodles are notorious counter surfers! Their long legs and keen nose give them an unfair advantage when it comes to finding tasty treats on your counters—and some of those tasty treats can make her very sick or kill her. Keep your kitchen counters clear of anything that your Goldendoodle can ingest. The basket of grapes left on the counter as an after school snack for the kids can land your Goldendoodle in the emergency veterinary hospital with possible kidney failure. And remember, depending on

YOUR HOME

Check your fencing and make sure it goes completely to the ground. You would be amazed at how small a gap a puppy can squeeze through; they can flatten just like a pancake! In fact, I recommend keeping puppies tethered (with you in constant attendance—never leave your puppy unattended) even if the backyard is fenced, until they are fairly reliable on the recall. Check the fence line regularly for signs of digging.

how far your Goldendoodle can stretch, just placing things at the back of the counter may not be enough to stop her. (Counter Surfing solutions are discussed on page 80.)

• Lock up your dirty laundry. You know that basket of stinky laundry? It smells like a buffet to your dog! It is amazing how many dogs make a snack out of dirty underwear or smelly socks. Sometimes they come out the other end . . . and sometimes they don't. When they don't, it creates a medical emergency for your dog and a financial emergency for your wallet.

• Check your yard products: fertilizers, pesticides, and herbicides can be very toxic to your pets.

• Keep all medications and chemicals securely hidden. Dogs can counter-cruise, and a simple bottle of pain reliever consumed by a curious pup can have fatal consequences. This is important in your house, your shed, and your garage. Even if you don't think your puppy will ever be

in these areas, clean them up anyway. Puppies are quick, and the last thing you want is your pup slipping out the door into the garage and lapping up antifreeze, because it is almost always fatal.

• Bathrooms! Bathrooms are another high-risk danger zone for puppies. With so many interesting-looking bottles of medications, bathroom supplies, and cleaning supplies, a puppy's curiosity could get her into a sticky situation. Keep these items up high and out of reach. And keep the lid down on the toilet. You don't want your puppy drinking from the toilet or, worse, falling in headfirst and drowning.

• Don't forget the tail. Not all puppy damage is done by puppy chewing. Make sure all breakable items are above tail level.

Bottom line? You must watch your puppy constantly. If you can't, put her in her kennel, out of harm's way. Anything she chews and swallows, other than her food, has the potential to make her sick or, worse yet, kill her.

YOUR GOLDENDOODLE IS FINALLY HOME!

You are on your way to pick up your new Goldendoodle puppy. Then what? This chapter will help you ease your new puppy into her new life with you and your family.

Bringing Home Your New Bundle of Fur

Transporting Your Puppy Home

As tempting as it may be, do not transport your new Goldendoodle home on your lap. It is best to transport your new puppy in a small kennel or carrier secured by a seat belt or a bungee cord. Unrestrained puppies, like children, can become projectiles if there is an accident or even a sudden stomp on the brakes.

On the trip home, expect your little Goldendoodle to cry . . . a lot! She has just been taken from everything she knows, so naturally she is scared and lonely. The crying subsides as she gets used to you, your family, and her new surroundings.

If you travel a distance to get your Goldendoodle, avoid rest stops. Your new puppy is not fully vaccinated and therefore is not fully protected from various canine diseases. If you cannot avoid rest stops, bring along a supply of large puppy training pads or paper tablecloths and confine her to them when you stop. To let her walk anywhere other dogs walk or eliminate is to put her at risk for potentially deadly diseases, the worst of which is parvovirus.

Bring along an empty bottle to fill with water at the breeder's kennel. Sudden changes in water can upset your puppy's young digestive track. If you have a very long drive, feed her only her normal food. That being said, chances are good your puppy will get carsick on the ride home. This is normal, and you need not become overly concerned.

What's in a Name?

Your new Goldendoodle will need an identity all her own. Give her a fairly simple name, preferable no longer than two syllables. Use her name often, but only in a happy tone. She will eventually begin to recognize the sounds you make as her name. Practice often, and every time she looks at you, reward her with a treat and/or warm, effusive praise. Never use her name when reprimanding her. You will use her name frequently when training and you want only positive associations with it.

Puppies Need Rest

It is important for the children in your home to have their play time with the puppy con-

trolled so she can get the proper amount of sleep. Like babies, young puppies need a lot of sleep in order to develop properly, both physically and emotionally.

Resist the temptation to take her to visit friends and family to show her off or have a parade of visitors her first week home. Let her settle in and get to know you and your family, her new pack, because even if your puppy seems fine and at ease (tail wagging nonstop, eating and eliminating on schedule), coming to a new home is intensely stressful for a young puppy.

Introducing a Puppy to the Rest of the Pack

Before you bring your new Goldendoodle puppy home, make sure your existing dogs are current on all of their vaccinations. The initial introduction to your other dogs is best done on neutral territory or in the backyard, because in the house there is the potential for territorial conflicts. If you have more than one dog, introduce them to the puppy one at a time. Now, even though they seem to get along, wait a couple of weeks before you leave the puppy and your other dogs unattended or alone together. When a new dog or puppy comes into a pack, there is often a honeymoon period during which the new dog is cautious in her interactions with her new pack members. After she has sized them up, her true personality will come out, and this can lead to unexpected clashes within a seemingly happy group of dogs.

At some point in her life, your Goldendoodle will probably challenge the other dogs to try to raise her status in the pack. They have to figure out their pack structure amongst themselves and it will get loud; your job is to make sure things do not escalate to the point of where the puppy becomes fearful or gets hurt.

Introducing a Puppy to Other Pets

A good rule of thumb is to keep all of your other pets away from the puppy. If introductions must be made, have the puppy leashed during the first several encounters. As she matures, her hunting instincts come into play during her interactions, which can lead to her suddenly chasing the cat she has, until this point, snuggled with or ignored.

Until she reaches maturity and her behavior is reliable, you must keep a close eye on her interactions with other species.

Where Should My New Puppy Sleep?

Choosing where your puppy will sleep can be a tough decision. Although you might not want her kennel to be in your bedroom long term, placing it next to your bed for her first few nights is a good idea. The use of the kennel is an important part of housetraining, and having it next to the bed allows you to hear her if she begins to stir and needs to go outside during the night. Once she feels secure and sleeps more restfully during the night, you can move the kennel to another part of the house.

Let Your Puppy Get Settled, and Be Cautious!

Again, give your new Goldendoodle puppy a good, solid week to acclimate to you and your family before friends come and visit. When friends do come, have them remove and leave their shoes *outside*. Canine diseases can unwit-tingly be picked up and transported directly into your home on the bottom of shoes.

Feeding Your Puppy

Feeding Schedule

You want to get into the habit of feeding your Goldendoodle at about the same time each day. This will help your puppy develop a routine and an internal schedule. The following is a general guideline for how often you should feed your Goldendoodle.

• Between eight weeks and four months you should feed your puppy three meals per day.
• From 4 months to 12 months you should feed your puppy two meals per day.
• For most breeds, once they are over 12 months of age you can feed one meal per day. However, as you will read in the next chapter, Goldendoodles are predisposed to gastric dilatation volvulus (GDV), a condition also known as bloat. It is better to feed dogs at risk for bloat smaller meals rather than one large meal. So, keep your Goldendoodle on a feeding schedule of two meals per day. The exception would be a Goldendoodle whose lineage has any history of bloat. This puts all puppies in that line at greater risk for bloat, and it is best to feed three to four small meals a day for the dog's entire life.

What Type of Food to Feed

The type of food you feed your puppy should be discussed with your Goldendoodle breeder and veterinarian. Be sure it is a diet balanced in calcium and phosphorous to support proper bone development. The canine digestive system can be very sensitive to dietary changes, so continue to feed your puppy the same type of food she was given at the breeder. If you want to change the food, do it very gradually by mixing the foods with increasing increments of the new food matched by decreasing increments of the old food. Watch your puppy and her stools carefully during this transition to make sure the new food is not causing any major irritations to her digestive system.

How Much Should I Feed?

There are many variables involved in determining how much to feed your Goldendoodle

Read the Fine Print!

Check your guarantee! If you purchased your puppy from a breeder, read your guarantee carefully. Many breeders specify a certain dietary regimen that must be maintained in order for the guarantee to remain valid.

puppy. Naturally as she grows you will need to increase the amount of food you feed her. However, take into consideration your Goldendoodle's predicted adult size.

The type of food you feed also makes a difference. The higher the quality, the less you need to feed your puppy. It is better to keep your Goldendoodle on the leaner side than on the heavier side, because obesity in dogs can cause a myriad of health issues.

It is always a good idea to have a conversation with your breeder and your veterinarian on this subject, particularly if your Goldendoodle has the potential to be a large dog. It is very important to feed large-dog puppies carefully to control their growth, because accelerated growth can result in bone deformities or weakness.

Who Knew Puppy Teeth Were So Sharp?

Biting and mouthing are normal social activities for young puppies when playing with their littermates, and your Goldendoodle puppy will naturally extend this behavior to her new pack members—you and your family. Unlike adult canine teeth, puppy teeth are needle fine and extremely sharp. It is important to teach your puppy what is and is not appropriate when it comes to using her sharp teeth.

Preventing Biting and Mouthing

The first order of business when training your Goldendoodle puppy is to inhibit the biting reflex. This is called bite inhibition. Your Goldendoodle puppy would normally learn her bite inhibition from her mother and littermates. However, because puppies are taken away from their mothers at a young age, it is up to her human family to teach her not to bite.

One great way to inhibit the biting reflex is to allow your Goldendoodle puppy to play and socialize with other puppies and well-socialized older dogs. If your puppy becomes too rough while playing, the other puppy will give out a very loud, sharp cry. It's through this type of socialization that your puppy learns to control her biting reflex.

TIP

Hands to Yourself!

It is important to never hit or slap the puppy, either during training or any other time. Why? Because physically reprimanding your puppy won't stop her from biting; it will simply scare and confuse her. Physical punishment is the surest way to erode the trust and respect that forms the basis of an effective training program.

TIP

Doggie Dental Care

Yes, dogs need dental care, too! Caring for your Goldendoodle's teeth is discussed later in this chapter in the grooming section.

Stop Biting Me!!!

It's relatively simple to teach a puppy bite inhibition by taking advantage of your Goldendoodle's retriever instincts. If your puppy wants attention from you, put a toy in her mouth before you begin to pet and touch her. If the toy is dropped, the petting stops.

If she does bite, quickly put the toy in her mouth. Should she drop the toy and bite again, give her a "time out." By denying her your attention and company, you are punishing her in a way she can understand.

Does the Tooth Fairy Come for Puppies?

As she grows, your puppy loses her baby teeth and grows her adult teeth. During this time, she needs to do a lot of chewing. It is important to have plenty of chew-safe toys available and for her to know which toys are hers.

Puppies will usually swallow their baby teeth, so you may find them in her stool. Occasionally you will find them on your floor—ideally not when walking to the bathroom barefoot in the middle of the night.

My Puppy Is Chewing Everything!

Puppies need to be taught what they can and cannot chew. If you find your Goldendoodle

puppy with something she shouldn't be chewing on, simply tell her "No," take the item away, and give her something appropriate.

Puppy Toys Must Be Durable

To be safe, your puppy's toys must be durable. If you notice a toy has been ripped, shredded, or has a chunk missing, try to locate all the pieces. If there are pieces and parts that cannot be found or accounted for, keep a close eye on your puppy and any changes in her stool's texture and/or frequency.

Playtime

Playtime is an exciting time for your Goldendoodle puppy, not to mention fun for you, too. Keep playtime fun and short, and end it before your puppy gets bored, distracted, or overstimulated. This will keep her enthused for the next time.

Appropriate Versus Inappropriate Games to Play

Goldendoodles are especially fun to play with, as they are joyful, eager to please, and always ready to participate in a game. Puppies learn a tremendous amount from play, particularly when you incorporate some of their formal training.

However, some caution needs to be employed when playing with your Goldendoodle, as certain games, although loads of fun for both human and canine, can teach your puppy the wrong lessons.

Tug-of-war and wrestling seem like relatively harmless and natural games, don't they? Unfortunately, these innocent games send all the wrong messages to your puppy, and neither children nor adults should ever play tug-of-war or wrestle with her. These outwardly innocent games produce feelings of rivalry and aggression, easily escalating to potentially dangerous situations later in the puppy's life

Playing "chase" teaches your puppy that it is acceptable to run after and jump on people. In addition, she learns that running away from you is fun, which is in direct opposition to her recall training.

TIP

Am I Ready for This?

Until she is fully immunized, your puppy is not ready for walks outdoors where other dogs have relieved themselves. It is critical to keep her within the safety of your own property.

Is My Puppy Possessed? No! It's the Zoomies!

Suddenly, one day, your darling Golden-doodle puppy acts like she's become possessed. She is running in circles at top speed, stopping occasionally to look at you with wild eyes, giving you a sharp bark, then returning to the wild-paced, circular running. Stay calm: Your pup is not crazy. Your puppy has the zoomies (also called puppy crazies). Just sit back and enjoy the show. Don't be surprised if this is a daily event lasting about 5 to 10 minutes. This is a perfectly normal canine behavior. However, it can be from a buildup of puppy energy, and you want to look at her exercise schedule to determine if she is getting enough exercise in her day.

Fetch, searching for hidden toys, and simple tricks are stimulating games for your puppy with the added benefit that they also teach her to obey you and your children, which reinforces good behavior.

Activities

How you exercise your puppy during her first year as she experiences rapid bone growth makes a difference in the long-term health of your dog's hips and/or elbows. Goldendoodles can be genetically predisposed to both elbow and hip dysplasia and too much exercise too early in life can cause long-term joint issues

for your dog. Moderate exercise, combined with a lot of play, is the perfect mix to keep your puppy happy and healthy.

Sidewalks and Roads—Not So Good!

Sidewalks and roads are very hard surfaces, and dogs under the age of 12 months should not exercise on them for long periods. The jarring force experienced when walking or running on a hard surface can, over time, have a negative impact on their bones and joints. Try to locate parks that have walking paths with softer surfaces or have your puppy walk in the grass adjacent to the sidewalk, road, or paved path.

If your Goldendoodle is less than 12 months of age, she should not engage in strenuous, forced exercise such as jogging or walking for several miles on a leash. Too much leash walking too early on can cause loose ligaments and fragile joints, leading to or aggravating hip and/or elbow dysplasia, as mentioned earlier.

Beware the Stairs!

It can be fun to watch your puppy race up and down the stairs, but this is an unnatural angle for her developing hips and should be avoided. Use gates to keep your puppy away from the stairs, and carry her up or down for as long as you are physically able.

Observe your Goldendoodle puppy closely to make sure her playtime, daily routine, and exercise do not consist of jumping off high objects. Something as simple as jumping off the sofa or the bed can, over time, have a negative effect on her joints. If she is allowed on furniture, invest in some pet steps so she isn't leaping off and landing hard on her front legs. This will help to protect both her hips and elbows.

Grooming

Whether you groom your Goldendoodle or a professional groomer does, it is important for your dog to get used to people handling her. If you do opt to have your Goldendoodle professionally groomed, be sure you are giving her a good all-over check at least once a month. Run your hands over her entire body, examine her pads, teeth, and gums, check her eyes, inspect her ears, and (yuck!) lift her tail to check her anus. It is important to know what "normal" looks and feels like for your Goldendoodle so that when something abnormal appears, you can recognize it and do something about it.

Grooming at Home

Regular Maintenance Unless she has rolled in something disgusting, your Goldendoodle will not need to be bathed frequently. If she is muddy, just let the mud dry and then brush her. That is the beauty of a Goldendoodle coat! Bathing too frequently strips the coat of its natural oils and can damage it.

If you are going to groom your Goldendoodle at home, it is best to do it on a raised surface. If you can no longer lift your puppy, consider using a ramp or stairs to get her onto the raised surface. This gives you better access to all areas of her body and it is much easier on your back and knees. Be sure there is enough room for your Goldendoodle to lie down, as it is often easier to trim nails when your dog is in this position.

Until you are confident your Goldendoodle will not jump off the table or try to run away from you (some dogs don't like to be brushed), keep a collar and leash on her.

Fur Depending on her coat type, your Goldendoodle's coat can be high maintenance. The curlier and softer the coat, the more prone it will be to matting and the more difficult to brush out.

Some Goldendoodles may need to be brushed every few days, others every few weeks. You will have to determine on your own how often you need to brush your Goldendoodle and how often she will need to have a professional grooming. If your dog's coat tends to fluff after brushing, squirt a little water on it.

I have found it best to brush in sections, working each section very thoroughly to remove any mats. Begin with the slicker brush and brush in short, firm strokes against the lay of the fur. Then using the wider side, comb each layer of hair in the direction it grows, and repeat with the fine side of the comb. Make sure you are getting right down to the skin so you are certain you have combed out her fine undercoat. It is this fine undercoat that causes mats.

Mats The Goldendoodle's fine undercoat is easily tangled and forms hard bundles of fur known as mats. Brushing your dog's hair thoroughly every few weeks produces fewer mats than brushing more often but not as thoroughly. Sometimes spraying the mat with a conditioning lotion first will loosen the mat and allow you to untangle it.

TIP

Brushing and Bathing

Be sure to brush out any mats before bathing your pup. Bathing will make the mats harder and tighter, and brushing them out will be nearly impossible.

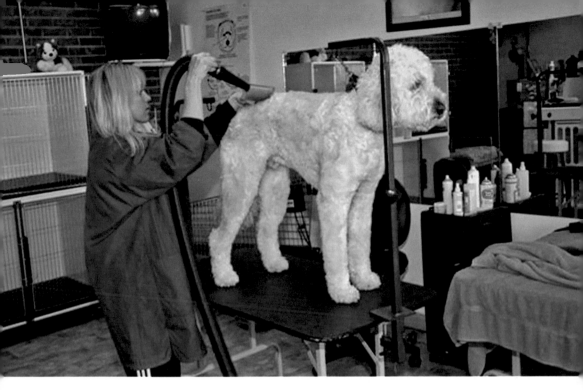

Keeping your dog mat-free is an ongoing battle for most Goldendoodle's owners, especially when your Goldendoodle is young. Your Goldendoodle's puppy coat will change to an adult coat somewhere between 9 and 12 months. During this time you can look forward to some shedding even if your Goldendoodle has a nonshedding coat, so expect to brush your Goldendoodle every few days during this transition period. Even with diligence, very often the fine undercoat becomes matted. This usually is the time most Goldendoodles get their first close clip or are shaved. The benefit of shaving her at this point is that the adult coat can usually grow in without the puppy coat and your Goldendoodle gets a fresh start.

Trimming Your Goldendoodle While the hair is fluffy from brushing, this is a good time to trim around the collar, neck, the ear flap near the cheek, under the elbows, between the hind legs, around the feet, and between the foot pads.

If your Goldendoodle is prone to ear infections, shaving close to the skin on her neck and under her ears allows for better airflow into the ears, which ultimately helps to keep the ears dryer. And if done properly, it is not visible unless you lift up the ear flap.

Trimming to keep your Goldendoodle's eyes free of obstruction is one of the first and most important trims you will do, and it is the location that should be trimmed most frequently. It is important for your Goldendoodle to be able to see her world clearly, because behavioral problems can develop if her vision is impeded.

Ears One of the reasons why we love Goldendoodles is their long, floppy ears. However, this ear structure also means they are very prone to

ear infections caused by restricted airflow into the ear canal. Additionally, with the retriever tendency toward waxy, dirty ears and the Poodles' tendency to have hairy ear canals, Goldendoodles are vulnerable to ear problems. Frequent cleaning with an ear cleaner will keep those ears free of waxy buildup and in great

---

TIP

Nail Trimming

I strongly advise having your veterinarian or the veterinary technician show you how to correctly trim your Goldendoodle's nails, particularly if her nails are black and the quick is not visible. If you are not comfortable trimming her nails yourself, you can bring her to either a groomer or the veterinary office for a trim.

condition to hear her favorite word, "*Treat!*" If your dog is very susceptible to ear infections, it may be necessary to pluck the hair in the ear canal. If not, simply keep the ears clean and trim the coat near the ears to increase airflow.

To safely clean deep inside the ear, use cotton gauze soaked in a solution of 40 percent vinegar and 60 percent water. Do not use cotton swabs in your Goldendoodle's ear. If you are unsure how deep inside your Goldendoodles ear canal you can clean, have your veterinary technician give you a lesson in ear cleaning during your next visit.

Dental Care There is a selection of canine dental supplies at the pet store to maintain the health of your puppy's teeth. To keep them pearly white, start brushing your Goldendoodle's teeth as early as possible. Brushing your dog's teeth once or twice a week is sufficient.

Most veterinarians will show you how to brush your puppy's teeth during your initial wellness visit. If this is not part of the wellness visit, make an appointment with one of the veterinary technicians for a quick lesson.

Feet If you are hearing a "click, click" when your Goldendoodle walks across a hard surface, it is probably time to trim her nails. Depending on how much time she spends outside wearing them down, her nails will need to be trimmed every 6 to 10 weeks. Keeping your Goldendoodle's nails trimmed to a correct and comfortable length is important to her long-term health.

Begin trimming your puppy's nails when she is very young. This often consists of just nipping the sharp tip off of the nail. Starting when she is young gets your puppy used to you handling her feet and hearing the sound of the nail clipper.

Use caution when clipping her nails. A dog's nail has a live center, also known as the quick,

TIP

Instructions for Your Groomer

The best grooming instructions I have ever seen for Goldendoodles is found on the International Doodle Owners Group's website: *www.idog.biz.* Just click on "Quick Downloads" then "Grooming Instructions," and print off two pages of precise instructions for your groomer. Along with detailed photos, there are boxes in each section to check off your particular preferences regarding the length of trim for each body part. This is an excellent tool if you are taking your Goldendoodle to the groomer.

---

which will bleed and cause your Goldendoodle pain if it is clipped. If your dog has lighter-colored nails, the quick is clearly visible and easy to avoid. If your Goldendoodle has black nails, look on the underside of the nail to try to discern where the quick ends. There should be a hollow space at the end of the nail.

Going to the Groomer

If you choose to take your puppy to a groomer, be sure your groomer knows this is a Goldendoodle and not a Poodle, or you could be in for a surprise. To be on the safe side give the groomer specific instructions, including what you want and *don't* want to be done. If you have a picture of what you want the final outcome to look like, bring it along.

If you plan for trips to the groomer to be a regular part of your Goldendoodle's life, start taking her early on so she can get used to the

noise and commotion of a grooming salon. When she is young, she probably won't need a coat trim, so simply take her in for a bath, brush, ear cleaning, and nail trim.

How to Choose a Groomer As with choosing a veterinarian, groomers are best found through referrals. If you see someone in your neighborhood with a Goldendoodle whose cut you like, ask them who does their dog's grooming. Because there are many dog breeds that require regular trips to the groomer, you can ask people in your neighborhood or at the dog park which groomer they use.

If you can't get a referral, ask the groomers in your area if they can provide any references from Goldendoodle or Labradoodle owners. (Labradoodles are trimmed in the same manner as Goldendoodles.)

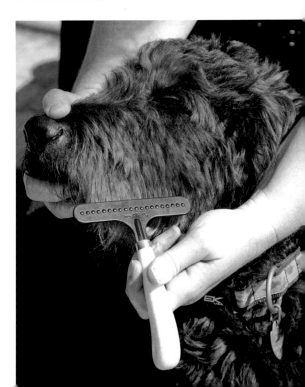

It is important to prepare your children for life with a puppy by teaching them the proper way to interact with her, and this means setting boundaries on their activities. If you teach them the right way to treat the puppy from the beginning, life with your Goldendoodle will be rewarding. Until she has reached maturity, you must supervise all interactions between your child and your Goldendoodle.

Young Puppies Will Bite

Until they are taught not to, it is very natural for young puppies to nip and bite; it is how they interact with their littermates. This can be painful and very disconcerting for children who may think that the puppy is being mean or wants to hurt them. You need to explain to your children that puppies naturally nip their littermates when playing and that your new Goldendoodle is not trying to hurt them, she's just trying to play.

It is important to teach your children how to behave when your puppy inevitably bites or nips them. You will make life less stressful for everyone by preparing them for a nipping puppy and practicing what to do before the arrival of your new Goldendoodle.

When a puppy nips, all play must immediately stop. The puppy is already in a state of excitement, so it is important the children avoid any high pitch screaming. I know this is difficult, especially if a child has just experienced the nip of razor sharp puppy teeth, but this is where practice and preparation pay huge dividends. Have the child pretend he is a tree and stand up as tall as he can while, at the same time tell the puppy *"No Biting!"* in a low, firm, authoritative voice. Once the child is standing, have him turn away from the puppy and put his hands on top of his head or under his armpits, out of her

reach. As she moves to face your child, have him continue to keep his back to her. At this point, if the puppy calms down, praise them both quietly and let them continue to play. If she is still in an excited state, it might be a good time for her to have a little quiet time in her kennel or go for a walk to get rid of some puppy energy.

Picking Up the Puppy

Children often want to pick up their new Goldendoodle puppy and carry her around as if she were a doll. Children should not pick up the puppy unless there is an adult present. The reason why? A puppy is naturally wiggly, and a child could easily drop and injure her or she can squirm away and be injured.

Have your child sit, preferably on the floor rather than on an elevated surface such as a chair, and put the puppy in the child's lap. To help the puppy relax and settle down, have your child give the puppy a chew toy. A young teething puppy chews on everything, including the young arms and hands of the child holding her. A chew toy gives her something besides your child to gnaw on and keeps her content in your child's lap for a longer period of time.

Children and Puppy Snacks

As parents, we're proud when our children finally learn the concept of sharing, but when you add a puppy to your family, all the rules about sharing change. Children need to understand that if they share their snacks with the puppy, it could make the puppy very sick, or worse, be fatal. You can avoid this by having a special jar of treats the children can give the puppy. Explain to your child that puppies can

get a bellyache from too many treats just like they can.

Helping to Care for the Puppy

Children should be given some responsibility for puppy care, although you should not expect them to be solely responsible. You should always supervise to make sure the task is done and completed correctly.

With your help, young children can carry out simple tasks such as feeding the puppy at certain times or filling a water bowl.

Make a chart for your children to put a sticker on every time they complete their assigned task. This makes it fun for them, and you can easily see whether their tasks are complete for that day.

GOLDENDOODLE HEALTH AND WELLNESS

There is a lot to know when it comes to good health and your Goldendoodle. In this chapter, we will talk about the basics of canine health care and give you the information you need for a healthy and happy Goldendoodle.

Your Puppy's Parents

Any discussion on the subject of Goldendoodle health needs to begin with a discussion about the health of the sire (the male parent dog) and dam (the female parent dog).

One of the great benefits of the Goldendoodle is the phenomenon known as hybrid vigor. This is when two different breeds reproduce with the resulting offspring getting all of the parents' positive traits and few if any of the bad ones. And this is true . . . to a point. Hybrid vigor is not the panacea that some breeders would like you to believe. As you will read in the next few pages, it is not a guarantee against inheritable genetic defects. If two different breeds carry the same recessive gene and are bred, trouble can result.

Hip Dysplasia

Golden Retrievers and Standard Poodles share a common and critical health concern: hip dysplasia. Hip dysplasia (also referred to as HD) is a structural abnormality of the hips, which causes the ball at the top of the thigh bone to wear against, rather than slide within, the socket in the pelvis. This wear creates a painful osteoarthritis in the hip joints. Surgery can often correct the problem, but it can be extensive, expensive, and painful. Although hip dysplasia is a hereditary disease, it can be exacerbated by rapid growth, poor diet, and exercise too vigorous for young, developing hips.

Responsible breeders screen their breeding dogs for hip dysplasia and breed only dogs whose hip scores indicate healthy hips.

Currently, the only way to detect HD is with an X-ray. The following organizations are the most commonly used to read and certify the X-rays.

OFA—*Orthopedic Foundation for Animals* (USA). OFA assigns a rating of Normal ("Excellent," "Good," "Fair"), Borderline and Dysplastic ("Mild," "Moderate," "Severe"). The official score can be obtained only from tests run after the dog is two years old. Before two years of age, the OFA scores are considered "preliminary."

PennHIP—*University of Pennsylvania Hip Improvement Project* (USA/Australia). The PennHIP system uses three different views of the hips (Compression, Distraction, and Hip Extended) to assess, measure, and interpret the laxity (looseness) of the hip joint. The earliest a dog can be PennHIP screened is four months of age.

BVA—*British Veterinary Association* (UK/Australia). BVA assigns a number to each hip, with the score being the sum of the two hips.

When looking at the hip scores of the sire and dam, here are some guidelines about where the scores should fall.

OFA: Good or Excellent

BVA: Should be 13 *or less*. Dogs with scores over 16 should never be bred.

PennHIP: .44–.55 is average. Dogs with scores of .6–.7 or higher should never be bred.

The bottom line is that all breeding dogs should be tested for hip dysplasia once they are old enough.

Be wary of anyone who tells you their breeding dogs' test scores are "Pending." Use of this term indicates they were bred before being tested and it should be considered a warning sign.

Other Parental Health Issues

Eyes The eyes are another feature of the Goldendoodle parents that should be tested in order to breed only the best sires and dams. This testing can be done through the Canine Eye Registration Foundation (CERF). This is an organization "dedicated to the elimination of heritable eye disease in purebred dogs through registration and research."

A painless examination is performed by a veterinarian certified by the American College of Veterinary Ophthalmologists who then completes a form and indicates any diseases. If the dog is certified to be free of heritable eye disease, you can send in the completed owner's copy of the CERF form with the appropriate fee.

Progressive Retinal Atrophy (PRA) is an inheritable eye disease that can affect both the Golden Retriever and the Poodle, as both breeds can carry the same mutated gene that causes PRA. PRA refers to a group of diseases that cause the retina of the eye to degenerate. Depending on the type of PRA, this can happen slowly over time (Slow Progression PRA) or very quickly (Rapid Progression PRA). In either case, the result is declining vision and eventual blindness. The mode of inheritance for PRA is, in most cases, an autosomal recessive gene, requiring both parent dogs to carry the gene in order for the disease to be passed on to their young. Fortunately, there is now DNA testing available to breeders which identifies dogs who carry the gene for one version of PRA, *prcd*-PRA.

von Willebrand Disease (vWD) von Willebrand disease (vWD) is an inherited bleeding disorder common in Poodles and, to a lesser degree, Golden Retrievers. It is similar in nature to the human bleeding disorder hemophilia.

The mode of inheritance for von Willebrand disease is an autosomal dominant gene, requiring only one parent dog to carry the gene in order for the disease to be passed on to their young. Testing for von Willebrand's disease is done by measuring the von Willebrand's factor in a blood sample or, in the case of the Poodle parent, by checking the DNA.

The parents of your Goldendoodle should both be cleared of this bleeding disorder before breeding.

Elbow Dysplasia Elbow dysplasia is a concern in Poodles and Golden Retrievers. Elbow dysplasia, like hip dysplasia, is a polygenic condition, meaning an unknown number of genes control it; however, the expression of those genes can be influenced by several factors, including breed, rate of growth, nutrition, exercise, and gender. The Orthopedic Foundation for Animals offers a scoring system and database for elbow dysplasia.

Gastric Dilatation Volvulus (GDV) Gastric dilatation volvulus (GDV) is also known as bloat. Deep-chested, large-breed dogs such as Stan-

dard Poodles and Golden Retrievers have a predisposition to bloat. You should ask your breeder if there are any familial tendencies toward GDV in either the sire or dam's lines. This knowledge allows you to take appropriate precautions with your Goldendoodle. There is no screening test available for GDV.

Your Puppy's Health

Locate a Veterinarian and Schedule an Appointment

Before you bring your puppy home, locate both a regular *and* an emergency veterinarian. Keep the phone numbers and hours for both clinics posted where they can be quickly found by any member of your family in an emergency. There is also a 24-hour, seven-days-a-week poison control hotline number: (800) 213-6680. You will be charged a small fee to speak with a professional, but this could save you time and even your puppy's life!

If you do not already have a veterinarian you trust, ask friends, neighbors, relatives, and strangers. (Just kidding! Sort of . . . Taking a

---

TIP

Be Clear and Concise

Clear and concise information about your Goldendoodle and her health is critical to your veterinarian, particularly in an emergency situation. It helps to create a list of symptoms and/or questions before you get to the clinic.

Questions to Ask Your Potential Veterinarian

✔ How long is the wait for a regular (non-emergency) appointment?
✔ How available are they for emergencies?
✔ How many years have they been in the community?
✔ How many veterinarians, veterinary nurses, and veterinary technicians do they have?
✔ Do they have a specialty? Some clinics are geared toward general practice, whereas others specialize in surgical procedures, cats, exotics, and so on. Make sure dogs make up the bulk of the practice.

trip to a local dog park and asking some of the dog owners there for veterinarian recommendations may lead you to a good veterinarian.) A call to a local animal shelter or rescue organization may also get you a few names worth checking out.

You also need to decide if you want a traditional or holistic veterinarian. Holistic veterinarians are gaining in popularity and becoming more widely available and may be more in keeping with your overall lifestyle. The American Holistic Veterinary Medical Association is a good resource.

If you are a first-time pet owner, it is a good idea to visit the veterinarian clinic before you bring your new puppy in for your first visit. It helps to meet the veterinarian and their staff, as well as be able to hear what an active clinic sounds like. To be honest, the noises distressed

animals make can be very disconcerting. It helps your puppy immensely if you stay calm during her first veterinarian visit, and knowing what to expect goes a long way toward being able to relax.

Your veterinarian and clinic staff are your partners in caring for your Goldendoodle. Always feel free to ask them any questions or share any concerns you may have about your Goldendoodle's health.

Schedule a preliminary examination with your vet for your new puppy. You will also need to schedule follow-up visits to complete your puppy's vaccinations.

The First Wellness Visit

Schedule a new-puppy wellness visit with your veterinarian within the first two days of bringing your puppy home. Bring along the vaccination and deworming schedule your breeder gave you. This helps your veterinarian determine what vaccinations your pup needs and when best to administer them. The veterinarian will also want a stool sample, so be prepared. . .

Until your puppy is fully vaccinated at 16 weeks, keep her in your lap or a travel kennel and avoid letting her walk on the floor when at the veterinarian. Without the full complement of their vaccinations, puppies are vulnerable to disease and need to be protected. Remember, this is the place where people bring their sick animals, and even the cleanest of clinics do not disinfect their floors between every patient. So, carry your puppy, but keep her on a leash in case she twists away from you.

During your puppy's first visit, the veterinary technician will get some basic information about your puppy, give her a look-over, ooh

and aah, take her temperature, and then take your stool sample to their lab for analysis. The veterinarian will then come in and give your puppy a thorough examination, her next round of shots, and worming medication. The veterinarian may ask you to restrain your dog for her exam. Some veterinary clinics will take your puppy into their "staff only" area to administer shots or draw blood. The reason behind this is so the owner's anxiety isn't conveyed to the puppy and there are other experienced staff members available to help.

Deworming and Vaccinations

Vaccinations

Your puppy should have received her first round of core vaccines at six to eight weeks of age, before you brought her home. The three preventable diseases, which are considered core vaccines, are parvovirus, canine distemper and infectious canine hepatitis. These are routinely vaccinated against to maintain good health.

Noncore vaccines are often dependent upon where you live and your dog's lifestyle. They include leptospirosis, coronavirus, canine parainfluenza and Bordetella bronchiseptica (both are causes of "kennel cough"), and Borrelia burgdorferi (causes Lyme disease). Consult with your veterinarian to select the proper vaccines for your Goldendoodle.

Rabies vaccines are required by law, and the frequency will be determined by your local regulations.

Deworming

Your breeder should take care of the preliminary deworming. Deworming should take place at two weeks and be repeated at four, six, and eight weeks of age. Worms are discussed in more detail later in this chapter.

Spay and Neuter

Spaying and neutering not only prevent unwanted puppies, but also help prevent certain adult afflictions, including pyometra (an abscessed, infected uterus) and mammary cancer in females, and reduces the risk of diabetes in males. There are also behavioral benefits, as neutered males are less likely to be aggressive.

Spaying and neutering are generally done around the age of 6 months, but can be done as early as 6–12 weeks of age (pediatric spay/neuter). Some Goldendoodle breeders spay/neuter their puppies before they go to their new owners. This is a positive step that prevents dishonest people from using these puppies as part of their puppy mill or backyard breeding business. However, there are some potential drawbacks to pediatric spay/neuter. It can cause spay incontinence in some female dogs. Also, because the sexual hormones interact with the growth hormones, physical differences can occur in dogs neutered before puberty. They often have longer legs, flatter chests, and narrower skulls. These differences can put added stress on the joints and cause problems for active dogs as they age, especially dogs who participate in agility sports.

There is also the belief that you should wait until dogs reach sexual maturity and complete

their physical development. With these varied schools of thought about the optimal time to spay/neuter a puppy, and the need to balance potential health risks and benefits, it is best to discuss this in detail with your veterinarian and make an informed decision about what is best for you and your Goldendoodle.

Things to Check Regularly

The purpose of regular checks is threefold. First, it is important to know what is normal for your Goldendoodle so if something changes, you recognize it. Second, your puppy can be sick or injured, and because dogs are programmed to hide any weaknesses, you may not know there is a problem if you are not tuned in to your Goldendoodle and her body. Third, regular checks of your puppy and all her orifices and appendages desensitizes her to being touched, making it easier for you and your veterinarian to treat her when medical attention is required.

Those Big Floppy Ears

As mentioned in the Grooming section of Chapter 3, the Goldendoodle's ear structure makes them very prone to ear infections due to restricted airflow into the ear canal.

If you notice a foul smell emanating from your dog, it is likely a yeasty ear infection, canker, or mites. These problems become more common when wax and dirt mix with the inner ear hair. Check inside her ears, and if you see a buildup of dirt, clean them. Once the ears are clean, check the color of the skin inside the ear; if it is red and looks inflamed, your Goldendoodle more than likely has an ear infection and needs to go to the veterinarian.

TIP

Food Allergies

Ear infections can also be a symptom of food allergies. Allergies and how to isolate a food allergy are discussed later in this chapter.

Eyes

Make sure your puppy's eyes are clear and have a normal level of discharge. If your puppy starts to have large amounts of discharge or her eyes look bloodshot, there may be a problem. See your veterinarian.

Mouth

You want to get into the habit of regularly looking in your puppy's mouth to check her teeth and gums. Discuss with your veterinarian and your breeder whether you need to brush your puppy's teeth.

Her teeth should be nice and white without any plaque buildup. Plaque tends to build up near the gum line, so look carefully. If you see plaque developing, consult your veterinarian. Plaque can cause dental issues that can have long-term health effects on your Goldendoodle.

Your Goldendoodle's gums should be a nice shade of pink. Bright red, blue, or very pale to white gums should be brought to the attention of your veterinarian immediately, as each is indicative of a potentially life-threatening situation.

Stools (the unfun part)

Your Goldendoodle's stools should be firm but not hard. Loose stools can indicate many things, and it is best to bring this to the attention of your veterinarian.

Paws and Pads

Check your puppy's nails and pads frequently to make sure all are in good order. These checks get your puppy used to you handling her feet, which is very important when you need to trim her nails. Keep your pup's nails trimmed, as well as the fur between the pads.

Skin

Do an overall check of skin, looking and feeling for bumps and parasites like ticks and fleas. Being familiar with your puppy's body helps you identify anything in the future that doesn't seem right.

Bodily Functions

You might not believe me now, but when you have a dog, you become a keen observer of canine bodily functions and the resulting output. And if that isn't enough, you will discuss them, in detail, with other dog owners and consider it a perfectly normal topic of conversation. It is at this point that you know beyond a shadow of a doubt that you have become a bona fide dog person.

The Back End

A friend once told me, "Poo is the window to your dog's health," and I have found this to be very true in my many years living with dogs. Very often when you call the veterinarian concerned about your dog, it is because you noticed a change in the texture, frequency, or urgency of her bowel movements. And yes, of course, you have to bring in a sample. . . .

So, let's get into this less than pleasant, yet vital, topic.

Stools Your dog's stools should be firm, well formed, and consistent in shape and color, entering the world without undue effort. You will learn what is normal for your dog and will be able to notice when things change. Although most dogs have the occasional soft stool, it becomes a concern if they persist for several days.

Diarrhea A puppy or dog with diarrhea is at risk for dehydration and should be taken to the veterinarian. There are any number of causes for diarrhea, but it is always best to get your dog to

the veterinarian if it persists for more than a day. Watch for symptoms of an intestinal blockage, which is discussed later in this chapter.

Constipation If your dog is straining to have a bowel movement and is unsuccessful, she may be constipated. If your Goldendoodle appears to be in pain, there may be a blockage in her intestinal tract and she should be taken to the veterinarian as soon as possible. Symptoms of an intestinal blockage are discussed later in this chapter.

Flatulence Although we have all laughed and gagged as a dog's flatulence has cleared a room, it isn't normal for a dog to be flatulent on a regular basis. If your dog's flatulence comes on suddenly and is accompanied by diarrhea, abdominal pain, or a loss of appetite, you should get her to the veterinarian.

Scooting Contrary to popular belief, dogs who scoot their backsides on the floor or ground do not necessarily have worms. Scooting can have several causes, including worms, all of which cause irritation to the anal area.

If you see worm segments or something resembling rice grains on your dog's back end or in her stool, it is probably the source of the scooting and your Goldendoodle needs to get to the veterinarian for an accurate diagnosis and proper medication.

Another cause for scooting could be that your dog has ingested something she is having difficulty passing through her anus. In my many years of having dogs, blades of grass are the number one item to get stuck. Unpleasant as it may be, you decrease your dog's distress by helping to remove the offending object.

Last, the lovely, long, curly Goldendoodle fur we all love actually poses a problem in the rectal area. If fecal matter gets caught in the fur, it can create a foul-smelling and uncomfortable mat. I recommend keeping the fur trimmed fairly short in this area. If you take your Goldendoodle to a groomer, request a "sanitary trim" which takes care of it.

The Front End

Dog Breath Your dog's breath should not be offensive. It should have a neutral odor or smell lightly of food if she has recently eaten. A puppy's breath has a slightly sweet odor. Bad breath is an indicator that something is not right, and unless you know your dog recently ate something ghastly, chronic bad breath is cause for concern. Something as simple as plaque buildup on her teeth, which over time creates a host of health issues, can be solved by regular brushing. If the bad breath persists, see your veterinarian.

Vomiting and Regurgitation It is not unusual for dogs to vomit, because they have a well-developed vomiting center in their brain. Vomiting is typically caused by eating hard-to-digest

---

TIP

Anal Glands

Infected or impacted anal glands are a source of irritation that is relieved by having the anal glands expressed. This is something you can do at home (if you have the stomach for it), or you can have your groomer or veterinary technicians do it. Keep an eye out for any swelling at the base of your dog's tail, as this can be an indication of infected anal glands, which require veterinary care. Unless your Goldendoodle has been recently shaved, this is something you have to check by feel.

---

matter, such as grass, which irritates the stomach. However, like other bodily eliminations, vomiting can be indicative of a bigger problem.

It helps your veterinarian make a diagnosis if you understand the difference between vomiting and regurgitation. Technically, regurgitation occurs when food in the esophagus is expelled, appearing unforced and without retching. In simple terms, your dog simply opens her mouth and the contents of the esophagus flow out. In contrast, vomiting is the forceful emptying of the stomach preceded by retching and often drooling. By noting your Goldendoodle's physical state when she empties her stomach, you can give your veterinarian significant clues about the cause of her stomach upset.

Occasional vomiting is generally nothing to get too worried about, but you want to inspect the vomitus to see what your dog is bringing back up. You need to clean it up immediately and completely. Dogs being dogs, they will go back and try to eat it. If it is undigested food, your puppy may be eating too fast, so try feeding smaller, more frequent meals.

If the vomitus looks like coffee grounds (old, partially digested blood), contains blood, or smells like feces, get your dog to the veterinarian immediately. It is possible your dog is suffering from a bowel obstruction and needs immediate medical attention.

Regurgitation is cause for concern because it may indicate an obstruction in the esophagus. If your dog is regurgitating, call your veterinarian immediately.

Projectile vomiting is a sign that something is very wrong with your dog. The most common reason is a gastric outflow obstruction; however, there are diseases that cause projectile vomiting, so call your veterinarian immediately!

If your dog is vomiting up clear, frothy bile, the causes can range from gastritis to an obstruction or bloat. Again, call your veterinarian immediately. The exception to this can be young puppies. Young puppies sometimes throw up bile when their stomachs are empty, usually during the night or first thing in the morning after having gone an extended period without a meal. Possible solutions are to feed her closer to bedtime, increase the number of meals she gets in a day, or give her a puppy cookie just before bed. If the problem persists (you guessed it!), call your veterinarian.

Motion sickness is also something that plagues many young dogs. The good news is that your Goldendoodle will eventually outgrow it. In the meantime, it is best to withhold food and water before traveling. Your veterinarian can prescribe a motion sickness medication for your dog to help ease her travel discomfort.

The Underside

Urination If your dog appears to be having difficulty urinating, needs to "go" frequently, or is having accidents in the house after she is housetrained, she may have a urinary tract infection. You should get her to the veterinarian as soon as possible.

Under the Hood

Bloat (GDV)—
A Life-Threatening Emergency

Gastric dilatation volvulus (GDV) is the life-threatening emergency commonly known as bloat. Bloat can happen to any dog, but typically, it occurs in those that are middle age or older. Deep-chested, large-breed dogs such as Standard Poodles and Golden Retrievers have a predisposition to bloat. Since many Goldendoodles often take on the structural anatomy of their Poodle sire, bloat is something every Goldendoodle owner needs to be aware of and take precautions against. The mortality rate for

TIP

Bloat

If your dog's efforts to vomit are unproductive, this can be a symptom of GDV, better known as bloat. Call your veterinarian immediately! I recommend familiarizing yourself with the symptoms of bowel obstructions and bloat; both are discussed in this chapter. Knowing the signs and symptoms may just save your dog's life.

bloat is high, with survival hinging on early recognition and treatment.

The Anatomy of Bloat (GDV) Bloat is often a two-part event. The first part is the *gastric dilatation,* in which the stomach becomes distended with trapped food, fluid, and gas. As the contents of the stomach ferment, the volume of gas increases, as does the dog's distress. The pressure from the expanding stomach then puts pressure on the other organs and the diaphragm, making it difficult for the dog to breathe. It can also compress the veins in the abdomen, preventing blood flow to the heart.

The second part is the *volvulus* (which may or may not accompany the gastric dilatation), in which the stomach rotates on its axis. Once the stomach rotates, the contents are trapped, the building gas has no place to go, and the blood supply to the stomach is stopped. With blood flow to the stomach cut off, the stomach can begin to die or *necrose.* Once the stomach

rotates, the dog's condition deteriorates rapidly.

Symptoms Typical symptoms of GVD are as follows:

• A distended abdomen, which, when thumped with a finger, sounds like a tight, air-filled drum. In the early stages, the abdomen may not be distended, but can feel somewhat tight.

• Pacing and restlessness, although, the dog may not look distressed

• Intense abdominal discomfort (possibly seen initially as a very "preoccupied" look on the dog's face)

• Whining or groaning when the abdomen is pressed

• Nonproductive retching or vomiting

• Pale gums and tongue

• Rapid development of severe weakness and shock

Risk Factors The tricky thing about GDV is although I can give you a list of risk factors, unfortunately, dogs without any of them can also succumb to bloat. I experienced this first-hand through the tragic personal experience of a dear friend. Her dog died from bloat and was the mother of one of my dogs, who is now considered at risk.

Hereditary and General Risk Factors

• Large, deep-chested breeds, a category containing both Standard Poodles and Golden Retrievers

• An anxious temperament

• Increasing age: Bloat typically strikes older dogs ages 7–12.

• Male dogs are more likely to suffer from bloat than female dogs.

• Having a closely related family member with a history of GDV. Ask your breeder if any of the dogs in your Goldendoodle's line have had GDV.

Dietary Risk Factors

• Feeding one meal per day

• Eating from a raised bowl

• Strenuous exercise on a full stomach

• Gulping food

• Drinking large quantities of water just before or after a meal

Treatment There is no home remedy for GDV. This is an acute medical emergency requiring immediate veterinary care. After a physical examination an X-ray is taken to determine if there is a *volvulus*, a rotation of the stomach.

If your dog is in the first phase of GDV (*gastric dilatation),* the veterinarian may be able to relieve the pressure of the gas by inserting a stomach tube. Next the stomach is washed out and, with the support of intravenous fluids, food and fluids are withheld for 36–48 hours. After this period, food and water are slowly reintroduced. Your Goldendoodle may or may not require surgery, depending on the level of internal damage caused by the gastric dilatation.

If your Goldendoodle is experiencing a full GDV, your veterinarian will determine if there is a possibility of saving your dog through surgery or if it would be kinder to euthanize her.

Prevention Nothing can prevent GDV. However, there are steps you can take to mitigate some of the risk factors.

• *Prophylactic Gastropexy.* This is a laparoscopic surgical procedure in which the stomach is surgically stapled to the abdominal wall (*gastropexy*). Although this won't prevent the buildup of gas, it allows for an easier release of the gas. More important, it keeps the stomach from rotating. If there is a familial history of GDV, you may want to discuss the pros and cons of this procedure with your veterinarian.

- Feed two to three smaller meals per day rather than one large meal.
- Keep your dog from bolting down her food. You need to slow the speed of her food consumption. This can be accomplished either by using a special bowl designed to slow down a gulper or by feeding her using a toy. A toy? Yes! There are quite a few toys on the market where you put your dog's food inside and she has to work at getting the food. This dramatically slows down her eating. (As mom to a gulper who is an at-risk dog, I can attest to the success of this method.)
- Monitor how much water your dog consumes before and after eating. She needs to drink, but keep her from consuming a large amount.
- Keep your dog quiet for at least one to two hours after eating. This may require kenneling her or, as in our case, kenneling the younger dogs who like to play with our at-risk dog right after a meal.

Parasites

They are repulsive and disturbing . . . and they are actively looking for your dog. Your vigilance goes a long way toward keeping your Goldendoodle parasite-free.

Roundworm

Puppies are often infested with ascarids, otherwise known as roundworms. From birth until 12 weeks of age, puppies need to be treated every 2 weeks for roundworm. It is advisable to have a fecal sample analyzed to make sure there are no other worms present, such as hookworm, whipworm, or tapeworm. If other worms are present, your veterinarian may prescribe a broad-spectrum dewormer. (Ongoing

parasite treatment varies, depending on where you live.) Work with your veterinarian to create a schedule of regular testing and treatment appropriate for your region of the country.

Heartworm

Heartworms are mosquito-borne blood parasites of dogs that can cause severe illness or even death. Prevention requires a tablet daily or monthly. Discuss with your veterinarian which option is best for you and your dog. Again, work with your veterinarian to create a schedule of regular testing and treatment appropriate for your region. For example, in a northern climate you may need to treat for heartworm for only about half of the year (mosquitoes don't fly in the cold!) but people in southerly locations may need to treat their dogs year-round.

Ear Mites

Okay, so how do you know if your dog has ear mites? Your dog will be scratching her ears, shaking her head repeatedly, or rubbing her head against anything and everything. If you see this behavior in your dog, take a peek into her ears. If you notice a strong, unpleasant odor and/or see a waxy, dark buildup, have your dog seen by her veterinarian. Your veterinarian will analyze the gunk in your dog's ear and give you an appropriate treatment plan. Cleaning your dog's ears on a regular basis helps to keep ear mite infestation and infections at bay.

Fleas

You want to be aware of fleas, because they can spread very quickly, especially in the summer months. Worse, they can infest your home! A female flea produces about 2,000 eggs in her four-month life span. These eggs fall off your dog and are hiding anywhere the dog spends time: in the ground, on her bedding, in the carpet, and so on. You will probably see the flea dirt (fecal matter) before you see a flea, so check your dog's skin closely, especially on her belly. Fleas can be prevented with a monthly treatment that results in fleas laying infertile eggs. If you notice your dog has fleas, consult your veterinarian to determine the best treatment and prevention.

Ticks

Ticks are another small bloodsucking parasite. During your first visit to your veterinarian you should talk about the types of ticks in your area and the best way to prevent the effects and diseases resulting from a tick bite. In many parts of the country deer ticks carrying Lyme disease strike many dogs and their owners. Tickborne diseases can be very serious, so tick prevention is critical. Products recommended by your veterinarian, applied on the back of the

TIP

Tapeworm

If your Goldendoodle has or has had fleas, keep a close eye on her stools for any signs of tapeworm. Tapeworms are transmitted to dogs when the dogs consume fleas during the course of normal grooming.

neck above the middle of the shoulders, will kill the ticks within 24 hours. It is critical that ticks be removed or killed within 36–48 hours before they can release the disease-causing bacteria into the bloodstream.

Diseases

Parvovirus

Your Goldendoodle is most vulnerable to a communicable disease such as parvovirus during her early months before her vaccinations are complete. You can help keep your Goldendoodle puppy healthy with these simple preventive steps.
• Keep your puppy in a carrier or on your lap while visiting the veterinarian and avoid letting her walk on the floor.
• Do not take her to pet supply stores until she is fully vaccinated.
• Begin training at home and enroll your puppy in a class once she is fully vaccinated.
• Keep your puppy away from areas where other dogs have relieved themselves.
• Socialization is critical for young puppies; however, make sure she socializes only with

How to Remove a Tick

Prevention is the best defense when it comes to ticks. Consult your veterinarian about the best prevention methods for your region and dog. Check your dog immediately after she is in an area where she could pick up ticks. The best way to check for ticks is by running your hands all over your dog, paying particular attention to the head, lips, ears, neck, and feet. Be sure to check along the edges of your dog's lips and ears, including inside the small indentation on the lower edge of the ear flap. Be sure to check inside the ear as well; ticks will crawl into the ear canal. If the tick is in the ear canal, your veterinarian needs to remove it. Most dogs enjoy being checked for ticks because it feels like they are getting special attention and a bit of a massage!

If you find a tick that has not attached itself to your dog, do not crush it. This can transmit disease. Drop the tick in a jar of rubbing alcohol to kill it. Dropping it in water or flushing it down the toilet does not drown and therefore kill the tick.

If you find an embedded tick, remove it as soon as possible.

Before you begin, you need a few items:
• Rubber or latex gloves (or something to protect your hands from disease)
• Fine-tipped tweezers
• A small jar of rubbing alcohol
• Antiseptic
• Triple antibiotic ointment

Anatomically, the head is the weakest part of the tick, and you want to keep it from snapping off and remaining under the skin. Contrary to popular myth, applying oil or petroleum jelly to ticks does not cause them to back out of the skin. It does suffocate them and, in the process, cause them to regurgitate and deposit more disease-carrying saliva into your dog. Touching the tick with a match or lit cigarette has the same effect.

There are three methods you can employ to remove ticks.

1. Once you have located the tick and have your hands protected, simply rub the tick in a fast, circular motion, maintaining your direction. After about a minute, the tick should back out of the skin. Pick it up and drop it in the jar of rubbing alcohol. This method may not work every time, but it is worth a shot, particularly if you do not have your tick-removal gear close at hand. Having the tick back out of its own accord will also be less painful and stressful for your Goldendoodle.

2. If the above method does not work, grab the tick with the tweezers as close to the skin as possible right where the mouth and head enter the skin. Do not grasp the tick by the body, as you may break the exoskeleton and release the harmful contents. Very gently, slowly, and steadily pull the tick. Be patient. Eventually, the tick will tire and loosen its grip.

3. There are various tick-removal tools on the market. If you prefer to use one of these, ask your veterinarian which one he recommends.

Again, do not crush the tick, as this can transmit disease. Once the tick has been removed, use an antiseptic to clean the wound left by the tick, then apply a little triple antibiotic ointment. A scab will form and the wound site may be slightly inflamed because of the irritation caused by the tick's bite. If, after a week, it is still inflamed, there may be an infection, and I suggest you contact your veterinarian.

other dogs and puppies who are fully vaccinated and healthy.

• Have visitors to your home leave their shoes outside. You don't know where those shoes have been and what diseases they may be bringing into your home. Until your puppy has all of her vaccinations, you need to be very cautious.

Kennel Cough

Kennel cough is the broad term given to a group of highly contagious respiratory diseases. If your Goldendoodle is going to be around other dogs, it is a good idea to discuss vaccinating her with your veterinarian. Most kennels and many obedience classes require dogs to be vaccinated for kennel cough before accepting them as boarders or class participants.

Other Nasties

Dogs can acquire any number of nasty bacteria or protozoa in the course of their life, and unfortunately, you can't prevent all of them. However, with vigilance, you can minimize the occurrences. Here are a few things to watch out for:

• As mentioned before, dogs can be disgusting in their choice of gastronomic delights. Make sure she isn't dining on canine delicacies such as the fecal matter of other animals or birds. These harbor an array of dangerous bacteria, as well as fungus.

- Keep your Goldendoodle away from the carcasses of dead animals.
- Don't let your Goldendoodle drink from puddles or streams. These are havens for giardia and leptospirosis, both of which can make your Goldendoodle very sick.

Caring for Your Sick Goldendoodle

Upset-Stomach Supplies

If your Goldendoodle has an upset stomach resulting in diarrhea or vomiting, it is always wise to have her seen by a veterinarian. If the veterinarian recommends a bland diet, the following items are good to have on hand:
- Canned pumpkin purée (make sure it is pure pumpkin with no other ingredients)
- Rice
- Ground chicken or hamburger

Cook the rice and meat thoroughly, draining any grease from the meat, and mix together in a bowl. You can store this in the refrigerator for two to three days. When you feed your Goldendoodle, give her a small amount of the rice and meat mixture, and mix in about a teaspoon of the pumpkin purée.

Taking Your Goldendoodle's Temperature

Your dog's temperature ranges from 100°F to 102.5°F (38–39.5°C) with the average being 101.5°F (39°C). Canine temperature is taken rectally.

Before you begin, clean the thermometer with alcohol and dry it off. Lubricate the end of the thermometer with a personal lubricant or petroleum jelly. Lift the tail and, with a gen-

TIP

Taking the Dog's Temperature

Until you get used to taking your dog's temperature, it is best to use two people: one to actually take the temperature and the other to ensure that the dog stays in a steady position of either standing up or lying down. A digital thermometer works best and is the easiest to read. Read the manufacturer's instruction to learn how it operates.

tle twisting motion, insert the end of the thermometer into the anal canal, then follow the manufacturer's instructions.

Once you are finished, wash the thermometer thoroughly and disinfect it with alcohol.

Giving Your Goldendoodle Medication

At some point in your dog's life, you are probably going to have to give her medication of some kind. Most canine medications come in chewable, beef-flavored tablets, and most dogs just gobble them up like they are treats. But what if your dog is prescribed a drug that isn't made as a yummy beef chewable? Or your dog is fussy and turns her nose up at the chewable tablets?

The old-school method has you prying your dog's mouth open, popping in the offensive pill, clamping the mouth shut, and stroking her throat until she swallows it . . . ideally. Frankly, this should be used as a last resort to get medication into your dog. I have never had a dog who enjoyed this. . . Would you?

———— T I P ————

Food and Medication

Remember that if you are using food to deliver medication, you will need to watch your dog's caloric intake, particularly for an ongoing medication.

If the medication is a chewable, beef-flavored type, the tablets can be cut in quarters so they are roughly the same size as kibble. Another alternative is to grind the tablets into a rough powder with a mortar and pestle, then mix it into her food with a spoonful of plain yogurt.

But what about the bitter-tasting pill? Your local pet supply store may carry a product designed to mask the bitter pill in a beef-or chicken- flavored wrap. They are wonderful! Just put the pill into the wrap, close it up, and give it to your dog. She thinks she is getting a treat.

Another alternative is hiding the offensive pill in a piece of cheese, bread, or meat. However, some dogs will sniff out the pill and refuse to eat it. Here is a way to get around your pill-sniffing dog. You will use three cubes of cheese (or whatever you are using to disguise the pill) to give one pill. Give your dog the first piece of cheese, which passes all inspections, then quickly give her the cheese with the pill while (and this is key) keeping the third piece of cheese right in front of her nose so she knows another yummy piece of cheese is coming her way. That middle piece of cheese with the pill in it becomes something she needs to consume to get to the next piece of cheese. This little trick works almost every time!

When Your Goldendoodle Is Recovering

At some point in your Goldendoodle's life, she will inevitably get sick and require special care and medication. The assumption in this section is that you have taken your Goldendoodle to the veterinarian and that all recommendations made by your veterinarian supersede any advice given here.

If your dog is ill or recovering from surgery, find a nice clean, warm, draft-free place for her. Take the opportunity to wash all her bedding so that it's nice and hygienic for your sick dog's return. If your dog requires more warmth than just household heat, discuss heating options with your veterinarian. For the safety of your dog, any supplemental heating needs to be monitored closely.

Your sick/recovering Goldendoodle should be kept quiet and calm, so place her in a quiet part of the house, away from noisy televisions and children. Educate your children to be gentle and quiet around the dog when she is ill or sleeping. You must balance the need to care for her with her need to rest and be left alone.

Feed your Goldendoodle a nutritious yet appetizing diet. Strike a balance, making sure it is tempting enough to make her want to eat but light enough not to upset her digestive tract. Your veterinarian may prescribe a specific diet, depending on what is wrong with your dog.

Remember, dehydration is a real possibility if your dog has had vomiting and diarrhea. Make sure she drinks water. If she won't or can't get up, try placing a bowl of water under her muzzle. Gently dip your fingers into it and smear the water on her tongue or gums. Sometimes this stimulates your dog to drink.

Spoon-feeding can also be used for water, liquid medicines, and nonsalty meat broths.

As your dog recovers, follow your veterinarian's recommendations for the resumption of her normal daily activities.

Allergies

Allergies in dogs are most commonly caused by biting insects such as fleas, airborne allergens, and food. Allergies frequently manifest in the skin and result in constant itching and scratching, which then leads to "hot spots" or open sores. The dog then licks the sores and, unfortunately, makes them worse. It is very important to work with your veterinarian to help find the source of the allergic reaction and to provide relief and medical care for the symptoms.

Food Allergies

Food allergies can be detected by starting your dog on a diet of limited ingredients, free of any preservatives, colorings, or artificial flavorings. Work with your veterinarian to create a diet that includes ingredients your dog has not had in the past. For example, switch to venison or lamb meat if your dog has always had chicken-and beef-based foods. There are a variety of hypoallergenic prescription diets available. When the symptoms are under control, various foods can be introduced, one at a time, in order to uncover what is causing your dog's allergy.

Atopic Dermatitis

Your Goldendoodle is at an unfortunate disadvantage when it comes to allergens inhaled or absorbed through the skin. Both Golden

---

T I P

Toxic Plants

Many plants common to our gardens and homes (including the dead leaves) can be poisonous to your Goldendoodle. Check the website of the American Society for the Prevention of Cruelty to Animals for a long list of toxic plants.

Retrievers and Poodles have a genetic predisposition toward atopic dermatitis, also known as canine atopy. This is a lifelong allergy condition that begins to show itself between the ages of one and three.

It all begins when allergens such as fleas, pollen, dust mite droppings, house dust, mold, human dander (don't laugh! I actually know a family whose dog is allergic to them!), and any number of other irritants are inhaled or settle on the skin. This provokes an immune response resulting in inflammation and itchiness. Because they are very sensitive, the ears are often the first area affected, and you may see your Goldendoodle scratching and rubbing her ears. Watery eyes, sneezing, and a runny nose often accompany active licking of the legs and scratching of the underside. As the scratch and itch cycles continue, sores can develop and lead to bacterial and fungal infections.

There are a variety of treatments that mitigate the symptoms; however, it is a lifetime affliction. Often the first recommendation is to switch your dog to a hypoallergenic diet to see if the reactions are food based. Failing that, further analysis is required to determine exactly what is causing the allergic reaction in your Goldendoodle.

If your Goldendoodle develops atopic dermatitis, it may be worthwhile to get a referral to a veterinary allergist.

Intestinal Blockages (Bowel Obstructions)

The first thing that needs to be said about intestinal blockages is . . . *pick up your stuff!* Goldendoodles are mouthy dogs, a trait they get from their Golden Retriever parent. They like to have things in their mouths. The number one cause of intestinal blockages is dogs and puppies ingesting things they find, often something smelly either stolen from the laundry basket or left on the floor. They find things everywhere and are known to eat just about anything that can be ingested. Since a dog's esophagus is larger than her digestive track, the probability is very high of an ingested foreign body causing a blockage in either the stomach or the bowels.

Symptoms

The intestine can become partially or completely blocked. Vomiting and a lack of appetite may be some of the first symptoms you see. A partial blockage can cause, over the course of several weeks, sporadic vomiting and/or diarrhea. If the blockage is complete, your dog may experience continuous projectile vomiting. She also cannot pass any stool or gas.

What to Do

Get your Goldendoodle to the veterinarian immediately. An intestinal blockage can be properly diagnosed only with an X-ray. If a

blockage is found, surgery will be required to remove it and repair any damage that might have been done to the intestine.

Toxic Human Foods— Yummy Things That Can Kill Your Puppy!

There are human foods that are very toxic to dogs. Chief among them are onions, chocolate, grapes, and raisins. It is very important that you make any children in your home and neighborhood aware of this. Here is a partial list of some of the more common toxic foods; your veterinarian can provide you with a complete list. Keep in mind that the toxic effects of some of these foods are not immediate.

• Chocolate—toxins: theobromine and caffeine. Both are cardiac stimulants and diuretics.

• Grapes and raisins—toxin: unknown. Grapes and raisins can be toxic when consumed in large quantities (9 ounces [252 g] or more) and can result in kidney failure.

• Xylitol—a common sugar substitute, causes hypoglycemia (low blood sugar) in dogs. It also causes acute and possibly lifethreatening liver disease. A very small amount is needed to produce toxic effects in your dog. Depending on the size of your dog, a single piece of chewing gum can be deadly. After ingesting xylitol, dogs can begin to vomit and develop hypoglycemia within 30 to 60 minutes. Some dogs will develop liver failure within 12 to 24 hours of ingestion.

• Apples, plums, apricots, cherries, peaches, seeds, stems, or leaves—toxin: cyanogenic glycosides. Cyanide poisoning can result.

• Onions or onion powder—toxin: Thiosuphate. Can cause hemolytic anemia, which is a breakdown of red blood cells that leaves your dog short of oxygen.

• Coffee grounds and beans, tea leaves—toxin: caffeine. Cardiac stimulant and diuretic.

• Wild mushrooms—toxins vary, depending on the mushroom. If you discover your Goldendoodle eating any mushroom you didn't pick up at the market, watch her closely. If any symptoms of illness appear, get her to the veterinarian immediately.

• Spinach—although not toxic to dogs in general, it can have detrimental effects on dogs with kidney problems. Spinach is high in oxalic acid, which removes calcium from the blood. Kidney damage can be expected, as the calcium is removed from the blood in the form of calcium oxalate, which then obstructs the kidney tubules.

• Macadamia nuts—toxin: unknown. A small quantity (as few as six) can cause accelerated heart rate, tremors in the skeletal muscles, elevated body temperature, and weakness or paralysis of the hindquarters.

• Tobacco—toxin: nicotine, which affects the nervous and digestive systems.

• Yeast dough—The dough will expand to many times its original size when it reaches your Goldendoodle's warm stomach. This expansion, and the gas produced, can be very dangerous for your dog. Since the Goldendoodle is, by virtue of its parentage, at risk for GDV (bloat), this large amount of rapidly accumulating gas can be deadly. The alcohol released from the fermenting yeast can also be toxic for your dog.

• Alcohol—Your dog is much smaller than you are and has a much lower tolerance for alcohol; therefore, she is much more vulnerable to its toxic effects.

Antifreeze

Be very careful when using antifreeze! Antifreeze has a sweet taste dogs (and cats) like, and a very small amount is enough to kill your Goldendoodle. Clean up any spills immediately and thoroughly. And, if you think your Goldendoodle has ingested antifreeze, get her to your veterinarian or emergency clinic immediately. There is an antifreeze antidote available, but it must be administered soon after ingestion. There are animal-friendly antifreezes available.

Seasonal Changes

It's when the seasons change that you really need to be tuned in to your dog. Watch her behavior and look for signs that she is uncomfortable. This becomes even more important as your dog gets older or if she's less than a year old.

Hypothermia and Frostbite

Keep a closer eye on your Goldendoodle once the temperature goes below freezing. The colder it gets, the shorter the time you should allow her to be outside. Once it goes below zero, she goes out, does her business, and comes back in the house.

My first suggestion is to let your Goldendoodle's coat grow out during the winter months. Keep her well brushed so she doesn't mat. If she is an older puppy, this can be a challenge, as the puppy coat is extremely prone to matting while it is transitioning to the adult coat. It's her undercoat that keeps her warm, so keep it in good shape. Keeping her nails, foot fur, and the fur between her pads trimmed minimizes the formation of painful snowballs between the pads.

If she is outdoors all the time (which I don't recommend for these very social dogs), make sure she has an enclosed and raised shelter where she is completely protected from the elements, including a heated water bowl that won't freeze. Provide lots of good soft bedding

TIP

Wet Coats

So what do you do about the snowballs that form on your Goldendoodle's legs in the winter? Break up the snowballs with your fingers as best you can, then just keep your Goldendoodle warm and let her drip-dry. Toweling her while there is still snow in her fur can create mats, so gently pat her dry as the snow melts. This would also be a good time to wrap your Goldendoodle in a blanket and snuggle. Watch your Goldendoodle carefully to make sure she is not suffering any ill effects from the cold. When your dog's coat is wet, it loses its ability to retain heat and keep your dog warm.

she can huddle down into for warmth and make sure no vermin can take advantage of her environment. Warmth, water, and food are magnets for mice, rats, and other undesirable critters!

For the indoor Goldendoodle, keep an eye on her feet when she goes outside to play or for walks, especially if you get a freeze and your neighbors are using salt and deicing products. Keep a damp washcloth near the door and wipe her feet off as soon as you get home. Salt can cause sores on the pads, and depending on the type used, deicers can be dangerous if ingested. Booties are always an option! Many companies today make great footwear for dogs.

If you have a very young or aging dog, or it is very cold outside, I recommend some kind of jacket, preferably one that blocks the wind.

like your dog is suffering from frostbite, wrap her feet (or the affected part) in a blanket or towel and gradually warm her up. Contact your veterinarian immediately.

Signs of hypothermia include violent shivering, nonresponsiveness, disorientation, and stumbling. Most cases of hypothermia are the result of the dog falling through ice. So if you are near a frozen lake, pond, or river, keep a very close watch on your Goldendoodle!

If your dog is showing signs of hypothermia, take her temperature. A dog's normal body temperature is 101.5°F (39°C). If your dog's temperature is below 100°F (38°C), call your veterinarian immediately.

If your Goldendoodle is suffering from hypothermia, you need to warm her, but not too quickly. Lying down with your dog and wrapping the two of you in a blanket is a good way to slowly warm her up.

Heatstroke (Hyperthermia)

Unlike humans, dogs do not sweat to cool themselves. A dog's primary method for cooling herself is panting and, to a very negligible degree, sweating through her foot pads. Because of their limited ability to cool themselves, dogs have a difficult time tolerating high temperatures.

Signs of Heatstroke

• The first indication that your dog has become overheated is heavy panting and labored breathing.
• Your dog may begin salivating heavily. The saliva will be thick and rope-like.
• Your dog may vomit.
• Mucous membranes and the tongue may appear bright red or grayish and pale.

Also, if your Goldendoodle has a longer coat, putting a sweater on her keeps the snow from gathering in her fur.

So what are the signs that your dog is too cold? The most noticeable one is lifting her foot up off the ground and holding it up. Check her ears and feet with your bare hand, because if they're cold, your dog is cold. Your dog may also start to shiver, a warning sign of possible hypothermia.

Watch for signs of frostbite. In dogs, frostbitten skin appears red, purple, or gray. If it looks

Protect Your Goldendoodle from Heatstroke

• Never leave your Goldendoodle in the car on a warm day. Remember, the air outside the car may feel pleasant and cool to you, but it doesn't take very long for the interior of a car in direct sunlight to heat up to dangerous levels for your dog.

• In hot, humid weather, limit your Goldendoodle's exercise. Choose the cooler parts of the day for a walk, and even if she gives you the biggest, saddest eyes, do not take her running.

• If your Goldendoodle is outside, make sure she is on cool grass and not asphalt or concrete.

• Make sure your Goldendoodle has access to shade and fresh, cool water. If you leave your Goldendoodle in the yard while you are away, make sure the shade is continuous and doesn't disappear as the sun moves across the sky.

• Your dog may appear to be disoriented or confused.

• Your Goldendoodle may have difficulty walking or even standing.

• Her rectal temperature is above 104°F (40°C).

What to Do

• First, move your dog into an air-conditioned building if possible.

• Call your veterinarian and make arrangements to transport your dog to his office.

• Take your dog's temperature every few minutes to determine when it has returned to normal range. You do not want to overcool her, because that creates a whole other set of problems.

• Begin to try to cool your dog. Use cool water on her legs and trunk. Do not use cold water or ice, as this causes the capillaries at the surface of the skin to contract and inhibit the flow of cooled blood. Use a fan to speed the evaporation and cooling process. This will gently cool the blood in the capillaries near the surface of the skin where the circulatory system then transfers the cooled blood to the core.

• Do not force your Goldendoodle to drink water.

• Heatstroke can bring on serious complications. Make sure your dog is not alone for any length of time until you can get her to the veterinarian.

TRAINING

There is more to training than sit, down, and come. How you interact with your Goldendoodle from the beginning sets the stage for her future behavior. A well-trained dog is a happy owner!

Advice from Edie

If you read nothing else about training your Goldendoodle, I want you to read the next two pieces of important advice. These are insights from my many years of living with and training large, active Golden Retriever mixes.

First, from the day you bring her home, treat your Goldendoodle puppy like she's a full-grown dog. What do I mean? Your cute, eight-week-old puppy quickly grows into a large dog, so don't encourage any behaviors you don't want in a full-grown dog. For example, it's cute when your new puppy jumps up on you to get attention. However, it's obnoxious and dangerous when six months later, your large eight-month-old Goldendoodle knocks someone to the floor.

My second pearl of wisdom is to be consistent. To be honest with you, it won't be easy; however, consistency pays huge dividends when you train your Goldendoodle. If you tell your puppy to sit, make sure she sits. Do not let her ignore you. You must gently, but firmly, follow through on your commands even if it doesn't seem to matter. Don't think, "I'll get her the next time," because by doing this, your puppy thinks listening to you is optional. This makes training your puppy more difficult and may put her in danger. Trust me, there will be times when it's critical to her safety that she obey your commands, so make sure it is not optional.

TIP

Dogs do not fail, owners fail their dogs. Your Goldendoodle looks to you for leadership and direction; your commitment to properly train her is one of the most important commitments you make, because it has a profound impact on quality of life, both hers and yours.

Who's the Boss?

Throughout the training process, your Goldendoodle puppy receives a great deal of attention from you. Just be sure not to give in to her demands. She will try to get your attention by barking, nudging, or jumping, but if she does, ignore her. Wait a few minutes, and once she calms down, play with her or give her a belly rub on your terms.

Puppies are demanding around mealtime, too, so feed her according to your schedule.

Behavior-Based Training

When your Goldendoodle puppy enters your home, she won't know right from wrong. The only way she learns it is through experience and training. If your puppy does something and receives a positive result, such as a treat or pat on the head, she will want to repeat that behavior. If she does something that gets a negative result, such as being ignored or scolded, she will not repeat the behavior. Now, it takes a few times for her to realize this, but with consistency, she will get the message. Consistency is the key to effective training. It is important that everyone in the home, including guests, understand and follow the rules set out for the puppy.

Positive Behavior

You need to teach your puppy not to chew on your shoes or eliminate in the house, but you also need to reinforce when she does something positive. For example, if your puppy barks to go outside, gently greets a visitor, or politely sits while you eat dinner, praise her. Use phrases such as *"Good puppy," "That's right,"* or *"Yes."* Make certain the praise is given immediately after the positive behavior so she makes

the association. This is called reward-based training, and it is an effective, fun, and compassionate way for your Goldendoodle to learn good behavior. I urge you to look for opportunities to praise your puppy, because it is a precious time of bonding between the two of you.

Negative Behavior

Negative actions such as digging through the trash, dragging a roll of toilet paper through the house, or raiding the clothes hamper are actually fun for your pup. Consequently, she will continue these actions until you teach her this is bad behavior. When you find your puppy exhibiting negative behavior, there are different ways to teach her that what she is doing is wrong.

1. Change of Focus One of the first things you can do is give your Goldendoodle a ball or a favorite toy to act as a distraction and redirect her behavior.

2. Verbal Reprimand Select a word you plan to use every time your puppy does something wrong, such as *"No," "Enough," "Hey," "Eh-Eh,"* *"Stop,"* or *"Wrong."* Do not scream this word, but rather be short, firm, and nonemotional—just enough to get her attention. Then physically remove her from the situation. Your puppy will soon associate the command with ceasing her current activity.

3. Ignore Her Ignoring your puppy is a challenge, especially when she is barking for attention, food, playtime, and so on. To ignore her, turn away, look at the ceiling, or leave the room. She eventually learns that barking doesn't get her the desired attention.

4. Time Out If your puppy behaves badly, give her a time-out. This can be tethered on a short leash, confinement to a small room, or being put anywhere there is nothing to play with or chew. Keep her confined for 30 seconds and then let her free, but only if she is not barking. If you leave her in time-out for over 30 seconds, she will forget why she is there. Repeat time out until she understands.

You want training to be a fun, cooperative experience for you and your puppy. If you put energy and enthusiasm into behavior-based training, you get a well-mannered puppy in no time. Just remember, consistency is the key to training success.

Crate Training

A crate is one of the best things for your Goldendoodle puppy, because it serves as a private den where she can retreat safely and securely. Here are a few positive benefits of crate training.

Benefits of Crate Training
• It provides a safe place to be away from others.
• It provides a place for good, solid rest. Uncrated dogs tend to be on guard duty.
• It facilitates housetraining because dogs are naturally reluctant to soil the space where they sleep.
• It makes for a comfortable bed and sleeping environment. It also prevents your dog from roaming the house at night.
• It serves as a temporary playpen when you are unable to monitor her.

How to Crate-Train
I strongly advise against placing the crate in the basement or some out-of-the-way place. Make it part of the family environment, and if possible, place the crate near you when you are

home. This encourages the puppy to go into it without feeling lonely or isolated. A good location for the crate is a central room in the home such as the living room or kitchen, or the

TIP

Crates and Emotions
Never put your Goldendoodle in her crate when you are upset or angry. The crate is not a tool for punishment. If you must crate her, make sure your tone is happy. Do not force her into the crate. Only good things should happen in the crate.

TIP

Do Not Use the Crate When

- your puppy is too young to have sufficient bladder or sphincter control for the duration of the confinement;
- the puppy has diarrhea;
- the puppy is vomiting;
- the puppy has not eliminated shortly before being placed inside the crate;
- the puppy has not had sufficient exercise, companionship, and socialization.

---

entrance to a large hallway. You may want to consider having more than one crate. Why? Have one in the kitchen for daytime use and another in the bedroom for nighttime use. Wherever you put her crate, give your new puppy a few days to get used to her new den and praise her every time she goes near it.

After family introductions, guide your Goldendoodle to her crate and have some treats or a favorite toy tucked inside for her. Close the door with your puppy outside her crate: The goal is to get your puppy so interested in getting inside that she paws and begs you to open the door. Now open the door, let her enter the crate, and praise her with words such as *"Good dog"* or *"Yes"* and lots of loving pats. Then let her out and ignore her. You want to downplay the exit so she doesn't interpret outside of the crate being better than inside. If she doesn't enter the crate right away, do not try to force her. At this early stage use only inductive methods. (The exception to this is overnight. You may need to place your puppy in her crate and shut the door upon retiring. If the crate is next to your bed, you can easily reach over and offer a reassuring word or a quick pet through the wire.)

Repeat this exercise several times, each time increasing the amount of time she is in the crate with the door shut. Your puppy may start whining, barking, or scratching the door. If this is the case, make her next confinement shorter. Again, you want this to be a positive experience. When your puppy has this routine down, start adding the word *"Crate"* or *"Kennel"* as she enters the crate. Soon, your puppy knows to go to the crate no matter where you are in the house.

After introducing your Goldendoodle to the crate, begin feeding her regular meals there, to reinforce the pleasant association. If your puppy readily enters, put the food dish in the back of the crate. If she is still reluctant to go inside, put the dish only as far inside as she will voluntarily go without becoming fearful or anxious. Each time you feed her, position the dish a little farther back in the crate. Once your puppy is standing comfortably in the crate to eat her meal, you can close the door. When you begin this training, open the door as soon as she finishes her meal. With each subsequent feeding, leave the door closed a few minutes longer, until she stays in the crate for 10 to 15 minutes after eating.

Spend the next couple of days practicing these exercises, and practice going in and out of the room while your puppy is in the crate, checking in every few minutes to get her accustomed to your coming and going.

When you let her out of the crate, quietly and calmly open the door and direct her outside to the designated potty area. Be sure to keep the crate close to the outside door, because if it is in the bedroom on the second

floor, your puppy will never make it outdoors before she eliminates. Repeat this process a few times before you leave for longer periods of time, and always make sure your puppy empties her bladder *before you go*. You may want to consider leaving a radio playing, as this creates a comfortable and familiar atmosphere for your puppy. Start slowly and build up to longer periods of time away from her.

Do not leave a bowl of food or water inside the crate while the puppy is unattended. That being said, if your puppy is to be confined for more than two hours, you may want to add a small hamster-type water dispenser for her.

Placing the crate in a temperature-controlled environment is also important, because you don't want your puppy to get too hot or too cold.

TIP

Crate Training and Discipline

Crate training promotes positive discipline and routine for your puppy. Teach your Goldendoodle (no matter what age) that the crate is the best thing in the world. Make sure every interaction your dog has with her new den is pleasant.

Cautions About the Crate

The crate serves as a wonderful training tool; however, there are some rules to keep in mind.
• The crate should never be used for punishment. Brief time-outs are okay; just don't verbally punish the pup.

• Be careful not to overuse the crate. This is not where your Goldendoodle should live. If crate time is excessive, your dog may not have enough time for exercise and social interaction with family members. Without this time, you create other problems such as fearfulness of people and new things. It may also cause aggressive behaviors.

• Never force your Goldendoodle into her crate, as this creates fear and resentment. Tossing in a treat is a much easier way to get her into the crate.

Separation Anxiety

If your puppy has separation anxiety, confinement may escalate the problem. Behaviors resulting from separation anxiety include
• continuous barking for 30 minutes or longer
• urination or defecation in the crate
• damage to the crate
• moving of the crate

• wet chest fur from drooling and salvation on the floor
• consistent destructive behavior when puppy is left alone
• following you from room to room
• frantic greetings upon your return

If your puppy has excessive separation anxiety problems, talk to a professional trainer about solutions.

Important Tips About the Crate

• Always remove your puppy's collar before she enters the crate, as it can get caught on the bars or mesh wire. If you must keep the collar on for identification purposes, use a safety "breakaway" collar.

• If your puppy messes in the crate while you are out, do not punish her when you return. Simply wash out the crate with a pet-odor neutralizer.

• Do not allow children to play in your Goldendoodle's crate or to handle her while she is in the crate. The crate is her private getaway, and her space should be respected.

Housetraining Your Puppy

Vigilance best describes the state you must be in when housetraining a puppy. Puppies need to eliminate after playing, eating, drinking, waking up . . . and anytime in between.

Cleanup on Aisle 5!

OOPS! Accidents happen! It is just part of owning a puppy.

As a new Goldendoodle owner, you quickly learn that your first priority is housetraining. Patience and vigilance are required during this process. Every puppy is different, and it can take a few weeks or several months for a puppy to be fully housetrained.

From the first day you bring your puppy home, train her to eliminate outside the house. Papertraining a puppy and then retraining her to eliminate outside merely prolongs the entire process and confuses the puppy. Dogs naturally develop preferences for going in certain places or on distinct surfaces like grass. However, if you don't proactively train her to go outside, she will choose a convenient place inside your home. The keys with housetraining are consistency and reward.

It is very important to know about how often your puppy eliminates. If she eats, drinks, or plays excessively, she will need to go more often. You must give your puppy plenty of opportunities to eliminate since she can't hold it for a lengthy period of time. One way to help you predict her need for a bathroom break is to keep a record of your puppy's urinating and defecating times for several days in a row. Start by determining the minimum interval between eliminations then subtract 15 to 20 minutes from this period of time and you have your puppy's temporary "safety zone." This is the duration of time she can generally be trusted to hold her urine after her last elimination (provided she doesn't drink a lot of water during this time). However, make sure you closely supervise her any time she is not confined to her crate or confinement area. If you see her beginning to circle or squat, scoop her up immediately and take her outside to the designated elimination area.

How Long Can My Puppy Hold It?

How long puppies can comfortably hold their bladders depends on their size and their age.

Generally speaking, at two months a puppy should be able to hold it for two hours. At four months, four hours; six months, six hours. And at seven months, most puppies are able to hold their bladders for eight hours. Now, if your four-month-old puppy can't go more than two hours without a mistake, then work within her schedule and provide timely potty breaks. (If your puppy is urinating with a great deal of frequency, this may indicate a urinary tract infection and you should contact the veterinarian.)

Consistency Is Key

Within the first couple of days your puppy is home with you, try to develop a sleeping, eating, playing, and napping routine to establish patterns for her. For example, you know your pup should always go outside when she first wakes up and before she retires to her crate. She should also go out within 30 minutes of eating, so scheduling meals at the same time every day helps you know when to let her out.

When you are about to take your puppy outside, say a trigger phrase such as *"Do you want to go outside?" "Do you want to go potty?"* or *"Hurry up!"* Say this phrase *every* time you take her out to help her make the association, and say it with excitement and a happy look on your face—even if it's at 5:00 A.M.!

It is also important when taking your puppy outside the first few times that you stay with her until she has done her business, because not all puppies completely empty their bowels or bladders on the first go. You may need to stay out a bit longer until your puppy has her second or third elimination, but you will get to know your puppy's habits fairly quickly.

When puppies go outside, they want to do everything *but* their business. With so many smells and interesting things to explore, your Goldendoodle is easily distracted, so make sure she associates outside with doing her business rather than play. To help this along, continually say trigger words such as *"Go outside," "Go potty,"* or *"Hurry up."* If this doesn't do the trick, try putting her on a leash and taking her

to the designated elimination area every time you take her outside. This way *you* control where she goes.

Praise and Rewards Work Like Magic

When your Goldendoodle eliminates, praise her in your regular tone of voice. Although you may feel like jumping for joy and loudly expressing how happy you are, don't, as it could startle her. Simply praise her and reward her with a treat the very instant she is done eliminating. Timing is critical. If you delay the praise and treat, you may be rewarding her for walking to the house, not eliminating outside. Praise and reward her every time she eliminates until she is fully housetrained.

Prevent Accidents

Here are proactive steps you can take to help prevent your puppy from eliminating inside.

No Access to Inappropriate Areas to Eliminate Whenever possible, keep your Goldendoodle puppy away from risky areas or surfaces such as rugs and carpeting. If your puppy suddenly runs out of the room, she may be looking for a secret spot to eliminate, so close doors to rooms where she may be tempted to do her business.

Supervise, Supervise, Supervise Supervise your puppy by keeping her on a leash, using gates, closing doors, and so on. Be alert. If she has frequent accidents in the house, she may develop a preference for those locations, which makes it harder for her to learn to eliminate outside. Every time your puppy eliminates in your house, it reinforces a habit—a bad habit. The puppy must be supervised at all times. If you cannot supervise her, put her in her crate with a sturdy chew toy.

Caught in the Act If your puppy is caught in the act, say in a loud voice (no yelling!), *"Outside!"* (once is enough) and whisk her off to her elimination spot outside. Then, in your normal, neutral voice say, *"Let's go outside"* or *"Let's go potty."* Guide or carry her to your preferred spot to let her finish. Do this even if it appears she is done.

Then ask yourself what *you* missed. Not the puppy; she is not to blame here, because somewhere along the line, you made a mistake and either did not follow the schedule or missed her cues.

After-the-Fact Discipline Does Not Work! Never discipline (verbally or otherwise) your puppy or dog for after-the fact house-soiling accidents you did not witness. Never. She will have no idea why you are angry and it will serve only to confuse her. Again, you are more to blame than she is.

Never Discipline Submissive Urination When puppies are overly excited, or feeling submissive, they can urinate involuntarily. Typical triggers of submissive urination are eye contact, verbal scolding, hovering over, reaching out to pet your puppy's head, animated movements, talking in an exciting or loud voice, and strangers/visitors approaching your puppy. Don't punish your puppy for this behavior or the problem could get worse. Don't worry; she will eventually grow out of it.

Housetraining Problems

If you find you are having a difficult time housetraining your puppy, ask yourself the following questions:

• *Did I leave her alone too long?* If "yes", take her outside more frequently.

• *Is the crate or room too big?* If "yes," block off part of the extra space.

• *Is she drinking too much water out of boredom or habit?* If "yes," consider giving her less water and involve her in activities to break the boredom.

• *Does she have a urinary tract problem or other medical condition?* If "yes" or "maybe," talk to your veterinarian.

Housetraining Signals

Using a bell or teaching her to speak are two very effective methods to help your Goldendoodle let you know when she needs to go outside.

Bell Method At the door where you take your puppy in and out for elimination, hang a small bell at the height of your nose. Each time you take her outside, physically take her nose or paw, ring the bell, then open the door. Your puppy will soon correlate the two and run to the door to ring the bell herself.

Speak on Command Another valuable tool to use, once your Goldendoodle puppy is housetrained, is teaching her to speak. When you are at the door, say, *"Do you want to go outside?*

Speak!" When she speaks, praise her, open the door and take her outside, then use the same exercise to go back inside the house. This is a great command for your puppy to learn because it can be used anywhere, at any door.

Obedience Training

Training is the most critical part of your responsibility for your Goldendoodle, because these are highly intelligent dogs who learn fast and need to be mentally challenged. It can also be the most gratifying part of your life with your dog, because a well-behaved dog is a joy. Does your dog have to be trained to perfection? No. She just needs to be trained to a level that works for you and your family. Your Goldendoodle will bring you years of satisfaction if you take the time and make the commitment in her first year to teach her how to live with your family and the community at large.

Obedience Classes

Obedience classes are important for you and your Goldendoodle because they teach you how to train your dog. Ideally they allow your Goldendoodle the opportunity to socialize with other dogs her age in a controlled environment. She also learns to focus on you and to ignore the other dogs and people.

Basic Commands

Begin training at home as soon as your Goldendoodle has adjusted to her new surroundings. Start with short training sessions and always end on a positive note. If she can't master a particular command, end the session with one she has mastered.

Come

Bend low or get down on your knees and say *"Come!"* Use a high, happy voice. As soon as your Goldendoodle reaches you, tell her she is a good puppy and give her a treat. Make sure she comes all the way to you, rather than reaching out to give her the treat. If she needs more encouragement, put on her leash and gently pull her to you. Practice this several times a day, each time increasing the distance, and she will soon come on command from any room in the house.

Sit

Stand in front of your puppy and hold a treat right above her nose. Say *"Sit!"* in a clear, low voice and move your hand back toward the puppy's tail. She will naturally lower her rear end to the ground. Once she sits, give her the treat and tell her she is a good puppy.

Down

Lure your pup into the sit position. Hold a treat in front of her nose and slowly lower your hand to the floor by her paws. As you do this, say *"Down!"* in a clear, low voice. If she does not lie down, move the treat *closer* to her body. As soon as she is all the way down, reward her with the treat.

Leave It

You will need two types of treats for this exercise. Place treat *A* on the floor. As she walks toward the treat, cover it with your hand and tell her *"Leave it."* When she stops, reward her with treat *B* from your other hand. Never give the *"leave it"* treat to her. You want to avoid training her that if she leaves it now, eventually she gets it. You want to teach her that *"Leave it"* means leave it forever.

Stay

Once your puppy can sit consistently on command, stand directly in front of her, hold your palm in front of her face, and say *"Stay!"* in a clear, low voice. Now take two steps back. If the puppy stays in her spot, immediately go and reward her. If she tries to follow you, say *"No"* and try again. With each success, gradually move farther away.

Common Behavioral Issues . . . and Solutions!

Jumping and Greeting Guests

I haven't met a puppy yet that didn't try to jump on people. This behavior can be cute when she's small but not when your fully grown dog has just laid someone flat or soiled someone's clothes with muddy paw prints.

Here's how the training starts: Before your company arrives, take your puppy for a good, vigorous, controlled walk. (If your puppy is too young for a vigorous walk, a good game of fetch to get rid of some of her puppy energy should do the trick.) You want to be in charge of the walk, not your puppy. No sniffing and exploring on this trip. This does two things: it uses up some of her energy and it establishes your leadership.

Next, when your company arrives, pick a spot to establish your puppy's company spot. This should be 4 to 5 feet (1.3–1.5 m) back from the door. Next, have your puppy in either her head halter or her collar with the leash clipped to it, and put her in a *sit-stay*, stepping on the leash so she can't get her head any higher than in a normal *sit* position.

Praise her for sitting nicely and give her a special treat you use only when guests are

coming. (Try some freeze-dried liver—disgusting to us but candy to dogs.) Have someone else answer the door while you continue to manage your puppy, all the while keeping her focused on the treats, her *sit-stay*, and your praise.

You can also develop a command for this activity. If you tell your Goldendoodle *"Company!"* she eventually associates her company spot and the desired behavior with this command.

It's just that simple.

Now I'll be honest: You need to practice this quite a bit before you can expect a calm puppy when people come into the house. So make people coming and going from your home a regular event rather than something special.

The other factor in this equation is how your guests react to your puppy. You can coach them so they change their behavior. When your guests first arrive, they need to ignore the puppy. Yes! I said ignore the puppy. This helps your puppy's behavior, because your guests are not reacting to an excited puppy. Calm begets calm.

Counter Surfing

The best way to prevent your Goldendoodle from stealing food from the counter is to not leave food on the counter. However, this is not how most of us live, and it is best to train your Goldendoodle to stay off the counters, if for no other reason than that some human foods can be fatal to dogs.

To begin, use a gate to restrict your dog's access to the kitchen. For the purposes of training, you want her to have access only when you are in the kitchen. Depending on her speed and temperament, you may want to have a leash on her. Now place something yummy on the counter. When she looks in the direction of the item, tell her *"Leave it!"* in a low, calm voice. If she looks away, give her a treat (something even yummier than what is on the counter) and lots of praise.

I would love to tell you that is all it takes, but if you have a very food-motivated Goldendoodle, you may need to employ more aggressive methods. Your dog is going to behave differently when you are not in the room, so if you are not there to tell her *"Leave it!"* she may still consider the chicken left to cool on the counter fair game. After all, you did leave it within her reach, didn't you?

If the first method doesn't work, you can try setting a booby trap for her. Take a cookie sheet and put a fistful or two of coins on it. Again, put something yummy on the counter, but this time place the cookie sheet in front of it, with it balanced on the edge of the counter. When she jumps up to steal the food, she will tip over the cookie sheet and be startled (but not harmed) by the sudden noise. This can often cure a counter surfer on the first try.

Not Coming When Called

Once she is trained to come, you probably won't have many problems with her coming to you in the house. In the house, you are the most interesting thing to her. Outside it is a completely different story. You immediately lose your status as the most interesting thing in her world.

The number one rule when your dog does not come when called is *do not chase her!* This may sound counterintuitive, but the best thing to do is wave your arms (dogs cue off of movement) to get her attention, call her in a happy, excited voice, turn around, and *walk or run away from*

TIP

Counter Pads

You can buy counter pads that deliver a small electrical shock to the dog if her paws touch it. I am not a fan of anything that shocks or zaps a dog, but if you have a real problem with your Goldendoodle counter surfing, you may want to look into one of these products. Or, preferably, put a permanent gate across the entrance to your kitchen.

your Goldendoodle. Practice this in controlled environments such as a fenced yard or, even better, a fully fenced dog park. Dogs are pack animals, and their instinct is to follow the pack

leader. A hand signal is helpful, as it allows your dog to identify you from a distance. Put one of your arms straight up, make a circular motion with your hand or full arm (depending on how far away your dog is), and continue to walk away, looking over your shoulder to check her progress. When she comes, praise her enthusiastically. If you are working alone, give her a treat, but, if you are at a dog park, treats invite trouble with other dogs, so effusive praise will suffice.

Socialization

A lack of early socialization leads to aggression, which in turn leads to a potentially dangerous dog. Many municipalities require any dog classified as dangerous to be euthanized. Puppy play is a very important part of their development, and most good training programs provide time in each session for this type of interaction.

Introducing your puppy to new experiences and new locations is also an important part of her training. Teaching your Goldendoodle to be obedient and responsive, even in the face of distractions, is very important when training her.

Get your puppy socialized right away!

Dog Parks

I highly recommend not taking your new puppy to the dog park. Not all puppies and dogs are prepared for such an overwhelming experience. Not only can this be potentially dangerous, scary, and counterproductive to your training, but your puppy can be stepped on, bitten, or rolled, leaving her with negative long-term effects. If your Goldendoodle shakes, shivers, or hides, this is your cue that she is not ready for

this type of environment. Generally, I recommend waiting until your dog is at least 12 months old before heading to your local dog park.

   If you have a miniature Goldendoodle, check to see if there is a play area for small dogs near your home. This gives smaller dogs an opportunity to play with dogs their own size.

Doggy Day Care

   Doggy day care is a great place to socialize your Goldendoodle. However, eight hours a day is too long for a new puppy to spend at day care, so I recommend starting with a half day, two or three times a week. Not all day care facilities are created equal, so before enrolling your puppy, visit a few and ask questions. Here are questions I'd want answers to:

- Is the day care clean?
- Are the employees educated and trustworthy?
- Are they licensed?
- Is there an area designated just for puppies?
- What is the employee-to-puppy ratio?
- What are their emergency procedures?

   Your puppy must have all her shots and be cleared by your veterinarian for these activities!

- Can they provide references?
- Do they have a webcam so you can see your puppy while at work?

Dog Walkers

   Hiring a dog walker to take your puppy out and play is another great way to socialize and train your dog. This keeps her on track with housetraining while you are away for long periods during the day. Be sure to interview and ask questions like the following:

- Are you the only dog walker who will be coming to visit?
- How long will you visit and play with my puppy?
- Do you bring other puppies over to play?
- Are you bonded and insured?
- Are you a member of a dog walkers' association?
- Ask for and call all references.

THINGS TO DO WITH YOUR GOLDENDOODLE

With her many intrinsic talents, your Goldendoodle has a world of opportunites open to her! This chapter explores just a few of the possibilities.

Your Goldendoodle is going to be a very smart dog and, depending on her temperament, quite possibly a very calm dog. The Goldendoodle's intelligence makes them perfect for just about any type of work or activity.

AKC Canine Good Citizen (CGC)

The Canine Good Citizen certification program was started in 1989 by the American Kennel Club (AKC). It is a 10-step test designed to test your Goldendoodle's manners at home and in the community at large. Passing the CGC is required if you want to pursue other canine endeavors with your Goldendoodle such as therapy work or search and rescue.

Therapy Certification Training

If your Goldendoodle has the right temperament (she must be comfortable around people and not easily startled), providing therapy dog services in a volunteer capacity to nursing homes, children's homes, hospitals, hospices, libraries, and other settings is rewarding work. Going through training to make sure she is suitable for this work is a must, and most states require certification.

Therapy dog certification varies from state to state, so by enrolling your Goldendoodle in a certification program you will be put in contact with the certifying organization in your area.

Search and Rescue

Search and rescue work requires an intelligent dog like the Goldendoodle and a dedicated handler; the training is intense and long, and the work is difficult, but it can be extremely rewarding. Search and rescue dogs are not used just for the big disasters we see on television, but also for the small, personal disasters such as locating a missing child or an Alzheimer's patient who has wandered from home. Your local police or fire department can put you in touch with a local training facility.

Competitive Obedience

Because of their keen intelligence and eagerness to please, competitive obedience is an area in which your Goldendoodle can excel. Once she has passed the CGC certification, she can participate in local competitive obedience trials, where her obedience skills (and your training) are judged. As she progresses, she can compete in more difficult trials.

Outdoor Adventures

Your Goldendoodle is an athletic dog bred from sporting dogs who spent their days in the fields retrieving game. She is going to be happy accompanying you on your outdoor adventures, so just be sure she is in the proper physical condition. As with people, it is never a good idea to take a couch potato on a 5-mile (8-km) hike.

Agility

Agility competition is a fast-paced race through an obstacle course where your Goldendoodle is off leash and directed through the course by you without the aid of food or toy enticements. Agility is physically and intellectually challenging for both you and your Goldendoodle, requiring a high level of teamwork and communication.

Tricks

Teaching your Goldendoodle to do tricks is easy and a lot of fun. You can either learn them from a book or, if your training facility offers them, take a tricks class. Either way, it is a great way to keep your Goldendoodle mentally challenged and your friends and family entertained.

CARING FOR YOUR AGING GOLDENDOODLE

As your Goldendoodle reaches her senior years, you will need to understand the changes in her care requirements. Being prepared helps her age gracefully and with dignity. And it will bring you many treasured moments.

I have a soft spot in my heart for elderly dogs. There is an inherent sweetness unique to an old dog. There is also a long history between you and your elderly dog; she has been reading your body language for many years and seldom needs instructions to know what you want or what is going to happen next. It is an easy, comfortable relationship.

The average life span for a dog is approximately 13 years, depending on the size of the dog and the care she has received throughout her life. When your Goldendoodle reaches eight or nine years old, she will be classified as a senior dog. Your veterinarian will likely change her checkup schedule from once a year to twice a year, because your Goldendoodle's health can change fairly quickly as she ages.

Good Nutrition

Good nutrition is important throughout your Goldendoodle's life; however, it becomes even more important as she ages. Work with your veterinarian to choose a diet to support your Goldendoodle as she grows older. Your veterinarian can also suggest supplements and other alternative treatments that can help your Goldendoodle maintain her youthfulness as long as possible.

Keep Her Lean

As she ages, your Goldendoodle is naturally going to slow down. This decline in activity needs a corresponding decline in caloric intake. Extra weight on a dog is never good, but it has a serious impact on a senior dog's health. Not

only does extra weight place added strain on her joints, but it is also an extra burden on her aging heart.

Exercise

Exercising an aging dog can be a challenge, because she may start her walk off at her usual pace, then slow down as the walk progresses. You need to be aware of how far she can go before she gets too tired. Trust me, it is no fun carrying home an overtired, old dog or trying to coax along an old girl who just wants to lie down in the grass and take a nap. Although it is important for your aging Goldendoodle to get daily exercise, it is equally important not to overdo it.

Behavioral Changes

As she ages, you will begin to notice small, gradual changes in your Goldendoodle. She will become less active, more sedentary, and sleep longer and more soundly. She may appear to be confused when awakened and be irritable if disturbed. She may also lose interest in all but her favorite activities.

Psychologically, your aging Goldendoodle is going to become less adaptable to change; alterations in her daily routine need to be made slowly. Visitors, particularly children, need to approach her slowly, handle her gently, and understand if she decides to walk away from them. Although your Goldendoodle may not want the attention of strangers, she will find

Traveling

When you travel, your old girl may be less tolerant of going to the boarding kennel, so consider having a friend come and stay at the house with her rather than boarding her. Staying in her home is a lot less stressful than being in a strange environment.

great comfort in being in the company of her family. Make sure her bed is near the hub of the family's activities.

Physical Changes

Physiologically, your Goldendoodle will have a lower tolerance for extremes of hot and cold, so it is important to place her bed in a part of the room where the temperature is moderate, consistent, and away from any drafts. Also, her aging joints may make negotiating stairs difficult. Because they are often unsteady, aging dogs can have difficulty navigating across wood, tile, or other smooth-surfaced flooring, so consider putting down a carpet runner for her.

As your Goldendoodle ages, her hearing will diminish which often makes it necessary to change from verbal commands to hand signals. Her visual acuity may also lessen over time, so if you notice her vision is failing, try not to move any furniture. She has a mental map of her home that allows her to move about without bumping into anything.

Your Goldendoodle's digestive system may become more sensitive as she ages, so make any dietary changes carefully and with the help of

your veterinarian. As she ages, health issues such as diabetes may require you to feed your Goldendoodle several times a day, rather than once or twice. Limit treats to only those of high quality, with a limited number of artificial ingredients.

Make Her Comfortable— Orthopedic Beds and Ramps

Geriatric dogs often need special gear. Orthopedic beds provide support for aging, arthritic joints. Also, depending on where you live, you may want to consider a heated bed for your aging Goldendoodle. Keeping her warm helps her mobility and improves her quality of life.

At a minimum, you will want to invest in a ramp to help your aging Goldendoodle move easily in and out of your car. This saves her joints from the impact of jumping and your back from the task of lifting her. If she is used to sitting on the furniture with you or sleeping on your bed, consider getting her a set of stairs so she can easily climb up and down. Though it may seem a very short distance from the couch to the floor, the impact on her front elbow joints can, over time, be debilitating.

Medications

As with humans, elderly dogs will often have one or two prescriptions along with several vitamins and supplements. It is important for everyone in the family to be clear about how and when these are to be administered to her. Write this all out and keep this list of instructions with the medications. An emergency may require a friend to feed and medicate your elderly Goldendoodle, and written instructions make it easier for you, your friend, and your dog.

INFORMATION

Organizations

American College of Veterinary Ophthalmologists
www.acvo.com
P.O. Box 1311
Meridian, ID 83680
Ph: (208) 466-7624
E-mail: office09@avco.org

American Holistic Veterinary Medical Association
www.ahvma.org
2218 Old Emmorton Road
Bel Air, MD 21015
Ph: (410) 569-0795
Fax: (410) 569-2346
E-mail: office@ahvma.org

American Society for the Prevention of Cruelty to Animals (ASPCA)
www.aspca.org
424 E. 92nd St.
New York, NY 10128-6804

ASPCA Animal Poison Control Center
(888) 426-4435
(There is a consultation fee for this service.)

Canine Eye Registration Foundation (CERF)
www.vmdb.org/cerf.html
The Veterinary Medical Databases—VMDB/CERF
1717 Philo Road
P.O. Box 3007
Urbana, IL 61803-3007
Ph: (217) 693-4800

Goldendoodle Association of North America
www.goldendoodleassociation.com

Goldendoodle and Labradoodle Breeders List
www.goldendoodle-labradoodle.org

The Goldendoodle Website and Forum
www.goldendoodles.com

International Doodle Owners Group (IDOG)
www.idog.biz

IDOG Rescue/Rehome Resources
Rescuing and Rehoming Labradoodles and
Goldendoodles throughout North America
www.idog.biz/IDOGRRR.html

Orthopedic Foundation for Animals (OFA)
www.offa.org
2300 E. Nifong Boulevard
Columbia, MO 65201-3806
Ph: (573) 442-0418
Fax: (573) 875-5073
E-mail: ofa@offa.org

University of Pennsylvania Hip Improvement Program (PennHIP)
www.pennhip.org
Administrative Center
3900 Delancey Street
Philadelphia, PA 19104
Ph: (215) 573-3176
E-mail: pennhipinfo@pennhip.org

Discussion Forums

The Doodle Zoo
www.thedoodlezoo.com

The Goldendoodle Website and Forum
www.goldendoodles.com

Books

Fennell, Jan. *The Dog Listener.* New York: HarperCollins 2004.

McConnell Ph.D., Patricia. *The Other End of the Leash.* New York: Random House, 2002.

Yin, Sophia. *How to Behave So Your Dog Behaves.* Neptune, NJ: T.F.H. Publications, 2004.

Important Note
Always use caution and common sense whenever handling a dog, especially one that may be ill or injured. Employ proper restraint devices as necessary. In addition, if the information and procedures differ in any way from your veterinarian's recommendations concerning your pet's health care, please consult him/her prior to their implementation. Finally, because each pet is unique, always consult your veterinarian before administering any type of treatment or medication to your pet.

Acknowledgments

My heartfelt gratitude to photographer Carol Vizcarra for introducing me to Veronica Douglas at Barron's Educational Series, Inc., and my deep appreciation to Veronica and Kristen Girardi, my editor, for making the publishing process easy and enjoyable. Ernie and Tahani, your unwavering love and encouragement mean the world to me. Special thanks to my friends and family for their steadfast support. Anni Boyum is the dearest of friends and a life coach extraordinaire. Her kind heart and wise counsel have helped me get out of my own way more times than I care to count. Beth Line, director of the International Doodle Owners Group (IDOG), is a wellspring of information, a valued friend, and an advocate for Doodles everywhere. Finally, warm puppy kisses to all my dogs, past and present: King, Clyde, Kayleigh, Sadie, Sonagh, Wally, and Murphy. You inspire me daily.

Dedication

In memory of my beloved Sadie. From the beginning, you were there for every word. Writing is not the same without you at my feet.

About the Author

Edie MacKenzie has owned hybrid dogs exclusively since 1985 and is one of the Web's leading writers on the special care needed when purchasing a hybrid or designer dog. She has written the following books: *The Definitive Guide to Labradoodles, The Definitive Guide to Goldendoodles, The Definitive Guide to Puggles, Your Doodle Puppy's First Year Made Easy,* and *The Perfect Little Training Guide for the Imperfect Owner.* She has also written numerous articles, many of which can be found on her website, *www. discoveringlabradoodles.com.* She lives in Minnesota with her husband, three dogs, and nine tortoises.

A Word About Pronouns

Many dog lovers feel that the pronoun "it" is not appropriate when referring to a beloved pet. For this reason, Goldendoodles are referred to as **she** throughout this book unless the topic specifically relates to male dogs. No gender bias is intended by this writing style.

Cover Photos

Front and back covers: Carol Vizcarra; inside front cover: Andrea Johnson; inside back cover: Lynda Blair.

Photo Credits

Janet Ayers: pages 49, 53, 69, 78; Kiersten Baker: pages 13, 16, 19, 20, 21, 22, 28, 29, 76; Lynda Blair: pages 9, 44, 56, 81, 82, 83, 87 (top), 89; Kent Dannen: pages 37, 71, 73; Tara Darling: pages 8, 30, 54, 68; Isabelle Francais: page 10 (top); Andrea Johnson: pages 47, 50, 66, 77, 80, 86; Connie Summers: page 10 (bottom); Connie Summers/Paulette Johnson: pages 2–3, 4, 32, 38, 39, 88; Carol Vizcarra: pages 5, 6, 7, 11, 14, 24 (left and right), 25, 34, 42, 43, 58, 61, 63, 64, 67, 74, 84, 85, 87 (bottom), 90, 93.

All inquiries should be addressed to:
Barron's Educational Series, Inc.
250 Wireless Boulevard
Hauppauge, NY 11788
www.barronseduc.com

ISBN-13: 978-0-7641-4290-1
ISBN-10: 0-7641-4290-9

Library of Congress Catalog Card No. 2009004420

Library of Congress Cataloging-in-Publication Data
MacKenzie, Edie.
  Goldendoodles / written by Edie MacKenzie.
    p. cm. — (A complete pet owner's manual)
  Includes index.
  ISBN-13: 978-0-7641-4290-1
  ISBN-10: 0-7641-4290-9
  1. Goldendoodle. I. Title.

SF429.G64M33 2009
636.72 |--dc22   2009004420

Printed in China
9 8 7 6 5 4